ARIZONA, UTAH & COLORADO

A Touring Guide

Larry H. Ludmer

HUNTER
PUBLISHING, INC

Hunter Publishing, Inc.
300 Raritan Center Parkway
Edison NJ 08818
(908) 225 1900 Fax (908) 417 0482

ISBN 1-55650-656-2

Cover: *Soap Creek, Colorado River, Grand Canyon, Arizona*
(Phil Deriemer/Adventure Photo)

Maps: Kim André

To my family
who never pressured me to stick with a "real" job
when I wanted to devote my time to writing about travel

Contents

Preface

Having spent a great deal of time traveling during the past 23 years, I have come to realize that there is nothing I enjoy more. Writing about travel comes close, so it's only natural for me to express a measure of gratitude to my editor who, more than anyone else, is responsible for this, my second book. Having taken so many years to reach the status of published author, it seemed to me that I had accomplished what I had set out to do when THE GREAT AMERICAN WILDERNESS: TOURING AMERICA'S NATIONAL PARKS was published. Now, at work on my fourth book, I am already looking forward to my next adventure in travel. I hope some of that excitement is shared by you the reader who will be using this guide as a planning tool for your travels.

Introduction

The adjoining states of Colorado, Utah and Arizona offer some of the very best vacation opportunities of any area in the United States. This trio is probably most famous for its outstanding natural beauty and recreational pursuits, but there is also a great deal of interest to those seeking out historical attractions, diverse cultures and cosmopolitan cities.

Colorado is at the heart of the Rockies. With a mean altitude of 6,100 feet (higher than every other state), over 50 of its peaks soaring to more than 14,000 feet, and even a "mile-high" city, few places on earth can compete with it for mountain beauty. And, despite its growing urban areas, you can escape from the hectic pace of modern life and discover the land as the gold prospectors did in the 19th century.

The state of Utah is like no other in many ways. It too is a mountainous place, but its mountains do not have the tranquil beauty found in Colorado. It is a place where nature has created unusual geological formations – arches, pinnacles, natural bridges and other wonders – of a strange, almost eerie beauty. The color of the land is as unique as its formations, adding to the immeasurable beauty here. Utah's history as well as its current society are also unique in America due to the strong influence that began with the Mormon pioneers and carries on today in this world capital of Mormonism.

The final member of the trio is Arizona. Here you'll find a diversity of natural wonders, with mountains, canyons and deserts. Add to that a history of Indian civilization going back more than a thousand years and the still-felt influence of the Spaniards who colonized the area.

Nature is not limited by the artificial borders we draw between states. The Colorado River, beginning high in Rocky Mountain National Park, runs through these states for some 1,400 miles. It then continues its journey briefly in Mexico, before ending in the Gulf of California. Not only does this river provide power and recreation for the people of these states, but it's the major source of the majestic scenery that makes the area a magnet for tourists from all over the world. No fewer than seven National Park Service areas lie along the banks of the Colorado, including one of the world's most famous natural attractions – the Grand Canyon.

Just as the river is a unifying force in this area, so too are the highways and backroads that thread through it. Several interstates and numerous other roads provide easy access to the majority of the region's most worthwhile sites. The chapters that follow will guide you on an unforgettable journey through these three remarkable states.

Getting Started

The chapters that describe the sights of Colorado, Utah and Arizona are arranged in three roughly circular routes, one for each state. Each route covers dozens of major attractions and many smaller, often lesser-known ones. The suggested itineraries for Colorado and Utah cover approximately 1,700 miles each and Arizona comes in at about 100 miles less. These distances do not include any alternative routes that you may add on.

You are not, of course, limited to the suggested routes. Information on deviations and variations is given at the end of each chapter. The circle route simply provides a framework for your trip. You may want to condense it, to lengthen it, or stray from the outline here and there. This will depend upon how much time you have and where your major interests lie.

Using the main route and the alternatives provided, you'll be able to cover virtually every part of these three states. But do keep in mind that, unless you're on an extended journey, it won't be possible to see everything in a single trip.

When to Go

Both Colorado and Utah are justly famous as great winter skiing destinations. Unfortunately, the snow, freezing temperatures and short days make winter a poor choice for anyone not on a skiing vacation. On the other hand, most parts of Arizona are simply delightful in the winter, with mild temperatures and bright, sun-filled days. Northern Arizona, including the Grand Canyon, gets its share of cold weather, though, and major snowfalls are not uncommon. So, unless you're limiting your trip to the southern half of the state, winter is not the best time to see Arizona. Of course, if you're just trying to escape from the cold and want to relax at a full service resort while taking in some of the local sights, Arizona has some of the best destinations in the country.

Spring is cool throughout most of Colorado and Utah and the northern parts of Arizona are very comfortable at this time of year. There are some drawbacks though – a late spring snow is always possibile and some roads at the higher elevations may remain closed due to snow cover until early summer. Also, many popular tourist facilities don't open until summer. If you simply want to get away from it all that may not present a problem. Late spring can be a nice time to travel (the crowds won't have arrived yet). Fall conditions are very similar to those found in spring. An added attraction is the fall foliage, especially in Colorado and northern Arizona. In Colorado and Utah, summer doesn't really come until the very end of June, or even later in the highest altitudes, and fall weather can come on suddenly in the first days of September. The same is true in the mountains of northern Arizona. Summer in the mountains is simply delightful. Sunny days with brilliant clear skies are the norm. Comfortable days are followed by crisp, invigorating evenings with star-filled skies. Few, if any, of your activities will be washed out by rain.

The lower altitudes and the southern "Dixie" portion of Utah are extremely hot, with temperatures in the high 90s or even higher. But the low humidity makes the heat easier to bear and cooler temperatures arrive with nightfall. Normal temperature ranges and rainfall for some selected locations are shown below:

	January			April			July			October		
	Hi	Low	Rain	Hi	Low	Rain	Hi	Low	Rain	Hi	Low	Rain
Denver	43	17	0.5""	61	34	2.0"	87	59	1.4"	67	38	1.0"
Grant Junction	35	17	0.6"	65	40	0.8"	93	64	0.8"	67	43	1.0"
Salt Lake City	37	20	1.3"	62	27	1.9"	92	61	0.6"	66	39	1.5"
St. George	52	29	1.6"	73	43	1.3"	100	68	0.8"	78	49	1.0"
Grand Canyon	41	17	1.2"	59	30	0.9"	83	52	1.4"	64	34	0.9"
Phoenix	65	38	0.6"	84	52	0.3"	105	77	0.7"	88	57	0.4"

Even in summer it is important to have a jacket for cool evenings and sometimes cool mountain days. Dress in layers year round so that you can adjust to the wide daily temperature swings in this part of the country.

Pack light. Unless you're going to be staying at a fancy resort or plan to dine at the very best restaurants, you'll find this a very casual area. Dress for the outdoor life and be comfortable!

Time Allotment

No two people will want to spend the same amount of time seeing a given list of attractions. But we do suggest a time frame of about 12 days for each of the main itineraries, based on the following assumptions:

• Maximum travel of about 250 miles per day, with the average mileage a very manageable 140 per day.

• An activity day beginning around 8 in the morning and ending at 5 in the afternoon.

• A "fast-food" or other fairly quick lunch.

• Sightseeing times at each attraction as described in the chapters. If no time is indicated it means most visitors will spend under a half-hour at the location. Hours of operation can be found in the Quick Reference Attraction Index at the end of the book.

Although many miles of driving will be done on fast interstate highways, this part of the country is dominated by slower, often narrow and winding, roads. Therefore, in calculating driving time, never assume that you will average more than 40 miles per hour unless you are on an interstate highway.

Lodging and Dining

Our objective here is to help you decide, not to decide for you. We provide information on areas with the greatest variety in lodging and dining along your route. The following are good sources of information on places to stay and eat:

AAA Tourbooks are the most comprehensive. Updated each year. Separate tourbooks for Colorado/Utah and for Arizona/New Mexico. Free to AAA members at any Club office. Mobil Travel Guides provide a good but less comprehensive list than AAA. You need the Southwest edition. On sale at nearly all bookstores and available in most libraries. Directories for major hotel/motel chains are available free at any property or by calling the toll-free reservation number. (See end of book for numbers and locations of major chains that are well represented in the Southwest.)

Pre-Planned vs. Day-to-Day Approach

There are two possible approaches to any sightseeing trip. You can carefully plan each day, allocating a certain amount of time for traveling, seeing various attractions, and ending the day in a pre-determined place with a room waiting. Or you can take things as they come, spending as little or as much time in each place as you want to and, when you've had enough at the end of the day, find a place for the night.

When you have a pre-planned itinerary you can be reasonably certain of accomplishing most of what you set out to do. This is important if you have a limited amount of vacation time and want to get the most out of it. With hotel reservations in advance you won't waste time looking for a place to stay or be confronted by "no vacancy" signs. That can be a real problem in out-of-the-way places where rooms are few and are quickly gobbled up. The advantage of the "day-to-day" approach is its flexibility. Enjoying a particular place? Then stay a little (or a lot) longer. For many travelers the planning stage is fun – it whets the appetite for the real thing. Others have difficulty in figuring out an itinerary or how long to allow for this or that. If you are good at planning, or even if you aren't, this book will provide the means for developing a successful plan, whether you follow the suggested routes to the letter or not.

You can combine the two approaches to some degree and here's how to do it. Decide where to spend each night based on the amount of mileage you want to cover each day. Don't allocate a specific amount of time for each attraction on the route for that day – use the ad hoc approach. There is some risk that you'll run out of time on any given day but if you do, you'll still have spent the most time at the attractions you enjoyed. On the other hand, if nothing appeals to you early in the day, you can almost always find something else to add on, so you won't risk getting to your destination at 2 o'clock in the afternoon with nothing else to do.

Some Final Words of Wisdom

The suggested itineraries begin in Denver, Salt Lake City, and Phoenix. If you're flying to your starting point, then renting a car, these are the logical choices because each is an important airline hub with a good selection of flights from anywhere in the country. A variety of car rental agencies can be found at or near the three airports. If you are taking a "fly/drive" trip, remember that the lowest airline fares apply to round-trip flights. Similarly, car rentals are less expensive if you return your vehicle to the renting station. One-way drop-off fees are often high, if the privilege is offered at all. Local car rental companies frequently have lower rates than the major national chains. So do try to make a loop even if you are not going to be doing the entire itinerary outlined here.

For those of you who live close enough to the route so that you can drive from your home, plan on joining the route at the point closest to your home. There is no reason to waste time and gas getting to "Point A" just because we've made it our arbitrary starting point.

No matter how carefully you plan, there is always the chance that you will get lost at some point. If you have good maps your chances of getting lost will be a minimal. The three state maps in this book are designed to provide an overall picture of your trip. Do not rely on them to find your way around. Bring a map of each state that you will be visiting (AAA maps are among the best, but official highway maps available from each state are also excellent). These maps should be supplemented with detailed city maps if you are going to be straying off the highways in larger urban areas and by maps of the National Parks that are available from the Park Service. Information on contacting these sources is available at the end of the book. We're now ready to begin our journey!

Chapter 1

Colorado: Heart of the Rockies

Colorado is the Heart of the Rockies for two reasons. First of all, it lies in the middle of the Rockies when viewing them from north to south. Second, no other state (except for Alaska) has as many towering peaks. Many of the most scenic western states are dominated by a single mountain or by unusual geological phenomena. More than half of Colorado is covered by an almost unbroken chain of mountains, each one competing for space as in a crowded urban skyline. Nowhere else in the United States is there so much "pure" mountain scenery.

But there is much more than the grandeur of nature here. Both Denver and Colorado Springs are large cities with plenty of cultural attractions to satisfy the most adamant urban tourist. Then, too, history is to be found everywhere, especially in Colorado's small towns – often living relics of a bygone era when gold miners came to seek their fortune.

Along the Suggested Itinerary

Denver is the logical place to begin our tour of Colorado. If you are arriving by air you will probably be flying into **Stapleton International Airport**, an important hub for several airlines that provides convenient connections from anywhere in the country. For those arriving by car from either the north (via I-25) or from the east (on I-70), Denver remains the best place to start. If you will be driving in from the west on I-70 you can pick up the suggested main route in **Grand Junction**; coming from the south along I-25 you can join in at **Colorado Springs**. As the trip is a complete loop it doesn't matter where you start

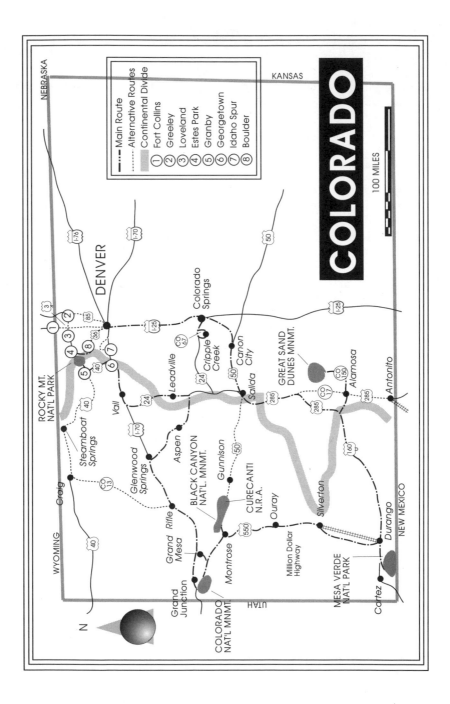

Stapleton Airport is approximately nine miles from downtown Denver. From the airport follow signs for I-70 westbound and take it to Exit 274. There you'll get on I-25 southbound for a short time to Exit 210. This is Colfax Avenue and the exit will leave you just a few blocks from the city center. An alternative route to reach downtown (which might be faster than the highway during rush hours) is to take Quebec Street south from the airport to Colfax Avenue. Make a right and head straight for downtown.

Before beginning our tour, let's get acquainted with how the streets run in the center of the city. Colfax Avenue is the primary east/west thoroughfare and is also designated as US 40, US 287 and Business I-70. The main north/south street is Broadway. The intersection of these two streets is the center of downtown and the beginning of the Civic Center area. East/west avenues are numbered (with Colfax being the equivalent of 15th Avenue) and have either an east or west prefix depending upon which side of Broadway they sit. North/south streets are named. The exception to this simple grid pattern is that the northwest corner of downtown has streets that run diagonally to the main grid. Here, numbered streets run parallel to the Cherry Creek which forms the western edge of downtown. Denver is a big city and you'll need your car (or bus or taxi) to get to some of the attractions, but the majority of in-city sights are located in the downtown area. As in any large city a car will be a burden here so park it and start walking.

Our downtown walking tour will begin at the **Denver Convention and Visitors' Bureau** located at 225 W. Colfax Avenue, just a block from the all-important Colfax/Broadway intersection. Here you can get brochures, ask questions on getting around, and find out about attractions or events that are taking place in town. At the corner of Colfax and Cherokee Street (a block west of the Visitors' Bureau) is the **United States Mint**. Due to limited capacity and generally large crowds, you should plan on making this your first stop to avoid the disappointment of being closed out. (Also note that the Mint usually closes for two weeks during the summer.) Guided tours lasting about a half-hour will acquaint you with the process of manufacturing coins and there is the opportunity to see a real gold bar. Walk back (east) on Colfax and you'll soon reach the impressive **Civic Center** complex. Located here are the **Denver Public Library** and other important municipal buildings, a monument to Denver's pioneers, and a veterans' memorial. There is also an amphitheater where various events are staged. At the southern end of the complex is the **Denver Art Museum**. Large galleries

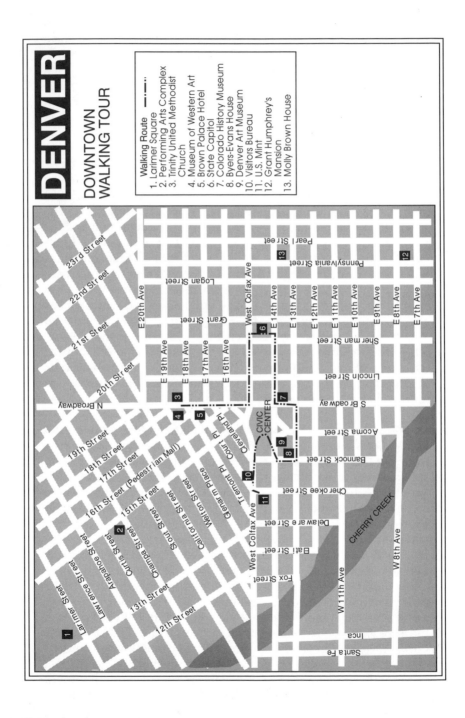

DENVER

DOWNTOWN WALKING TOUR

Walking Route ——·——·
1. Larimer Square
2. Performing Arts Complex
3. Trinity United Methodist Church
4. Museum of Western Art
5. Brown Palace Hotel
6. State Capitol
7. Colorado History Museum
8. Byers-Evans House
9. Denver Art Museum
10. Visitors Bureau
11. U.S. Mint
12. Grant Humphrey's Mansion
13. Molly Brown House

here contain art objects from the four corners of the earth, but many visitors will find that the structure which houses the museum is the main attraction. The building is faced with glass tiles and has 28 sides – try counting them! The Civic Center and Art Museum should take about an hour to visit, but allow longer if you plan to get a detailed look at the art collection.

Across from the Civic Center's southwest side at 1310 Bannock Street is the **Byers-Evans House**. This Victorian structure was built in 1883 by an important pioneer family and is furnished in period antiques. There are many other houses of this era throughout Denver and the number you visit will depend upon your interest in this genre. Byers-Evans is a good choice because it is representative of the architectural style, is conveniently located and the same building houses an interesting museum on the history of Denver. Allow 30 minutes for your visit. If you would like to see more of these Victorian homes, some of the better-known examples are the nearby **Grant Humphreys Mansion** (770 Pennsylvania Street, 1902), the **Molly Brown House** (1340 Pennsylvania Street, 1889, once occupied by a survivor of the Titanic disaster), and the **Pearce-McAllister Cottage** (1880 Gaylord Street; 1899, Victorian interior with doll and toy museum).

At 13th Avenue and Broadway (two blocks from Byers-Evans) is the **Colorado History Museum**. The museum's large collection traces the history of the state from before the arrival of pioneers by means of interesting dioramas as well as artifacts and documents. Give yourself an hour to stroll through and learn. When you're ready for some more historical sites, walk back to 14th Avenue, turn right and go one block until you reach **Colorado's State Capitol**. This impressive landmark building was built of native Colorado granite and is topped by a 180-foot-high dome covered with gold leaf. Rose-colored pillars grace the interior. The 15th step of the west entrance to the Capitol is at an altitude of exactly 5,280 feet, thus giving Denver its nickname of "The Mile-High City." Guided tours of the Capitol last almost an hour.

After leaving the Capitol, go back to Broadway, turn right and walk for three blocks to the **Trinity United Methodist Church**. This is Denver's oldest church and is well known for its Tiffany stained glass windows that were installed almost 30 years after the church opened in 1859. Small bulbs above the altar are meant to represent the 66 books of the Bible. You can visit the church on your own or by guided tour. In either case, expect to spend up to a half-hour here. Directly across the street from the church is another Denver institution – the **Brown Palace Hotel**. This world-renowned hostelry is on the National Register of Historic Places and dates from 1892. The popular "modern" architectural style of large hotel atriums may have come from the Brown Palace. Be sure to look up at the magnificent stained glass ceiling. Also, take time to relax in the plush lobby with its red leather chairs and authentic oriental rugs. If you decide to stay overnight at the Brown Palace it will set you back around $200 per night, but those who seek out luxury will tell you that the service here makes it worth the price.

From the Brown Palace it is just a hop, skip and a jump to the **Museum of Western Art** at 1727 Tremont Place. Here you can trace the history of the frontier as it has been seen through the eyes of virtually every major American western artist, including Frederick Remington and Charles Russell. A casual stroll through the galleries will take just over a half-hour, but allow at least twice that if you want to study the works of art in greater detail.

This concludes the walking tour of downtown (except for some of the historic shopping areas to be discussed later). Now it's time to find your car and start exploring other parts of the city.

Denver is rightly known for and proud of its many beautiful parks. Probably the most important of these is **City Park**, located between 17th and 23rd Avenues about three miles east of downtown via Colfax Avenue and York Street. City Park contains, besides the usual recreational opportunities associated with a major urban park, some lovely gardens that are enhanced by classic fountains and monuments. The park is also the home of two major attractions, the **Denver Museum of Natural History** and the **Denver Zoo**. The Museum is one of the largest of its type in the nation and has displays of dinosaurs and other ancient life forms as well as an IMAX theater and a planetarium. It will take most visitors at least 90 minutes to see the museum and that does not include time for the theater or planetarium show. The zoo has animals from all over the world and they are free to roam in natural settings that duplicate their native habitats. An indoor tropical rainforest called Tropical Discovery is of special interest. Allocate about an hour for the zoo and perhaps more if you are traveling with children.

Cheesman Park is three blocks south of Colfax Avenue via Franklin Street, which is approximately two miles from Civic Center. This park has fewer facilities than City Park, but it is well known for its attractive colonnade and portico which provides, on clear days, a panorama of the mountains that form a backdrop for Denver. In ideal conditions the view extends from Pikes Peak in the south to Mt. Evans in the north, a distance of almost 150 miles. Immediately to the east of Cheesman Park are the **Denver Botanic Gardens**. The gardens include a Japanese garden, rock and water gardens and a domed conservatory where more than 800 tropical and subtropical species are displayed. The gardens, including the conservatory, can be visited in about 45 minutes.

A far different type of garden is the **Elitch Gardens** at 4620 W. 38th Avenue in the northwestern section of the city. You can get there by taking I-25 to Exit 213 and then following 38th Avenue west for three miles. Here you will find more colorful flower gardens, but the site is more popularly known for its amusement park rides and entertainment. As with most such places the admission cost is fairly high. If you have children you may well spend several hours here and find that it's money well spent.

GOLDEN – DENVER'S SUPER SUBURB: One of the nicest things about Denver is that it is so close to the beauty of nature. The mountains are close enough that you feel as if you could reach out and touch them. Touching them can become a reality once you get to the western suburb of Golden in the foothills of the Rockies. The mountains rise abruptly from these foothills.

Travel to the vicinity of Golden by taking I-70 westbound (most easily reached from downtown by US 6) to Exit 260. Then take CO 470 to CO 74 at the small town of Morrison until you reach **Red Rocks Park**. This beautiful natural area has been turned into a 10,000-seat outdoor amphitheater where major concerts are held. The amphitheater is reached by a short but relatively steep climb from the parking area and is surrounded by soft sandstone cliffs that tower several hundred feet above the stage. The cliffs are a dazzling red color due to the high iron content and are a beautiful sight, as is the view of Denver's skyline from this area.

Leave the park through the northern entrance and take CO 26 and US 40 to US 6 west into Golden – a total distance of about eight miles. Within the town itself are several interesting attractions. First is the **Astor House Hotel**, another Victorian structure that was once an elegant place to stay. The hotel is located on 12th Street and has been restored to its 1867 appearance. On 13th Street is the **Coors Brewery**. Free shuttle service is provided from the parking lot to the brewery itself, where guided tours are given of the entire beer-making process. Allow about an hour for your visit. Next, on 16th Street, is the **Colorado School of Mines Geology Museum**. Besides showing the many minerals that are found in Colorado, the museum has a recreated mine from the gold-rush era. You can see the exhibits in under a half-hour.

Just east of town is the fine **Colorado Railroad Museum**. Take I-70 to Exit 265 and follow W. 44th Avenue to the museum. Vintage locomotives and other cars from the earliest days of railroading in Colorado are on display. There is also an excellent model railway collection. The entire museum can be covered in 45 minutes.

Perhaps the most worthwhile attractions of all in Golden are to be found in **Lookout Mountain Park**, about five miles west of US 6 by a winding, climbing, but easy road. The summit offers a panoramic view of Denver to the east and the magnificent Rockies to the west. It is in this splendid setting that William Cody, known to us as Buffalo Bill, chose to be buried. His simple but attractive gravesite can be visited. Adjacent to the grave is the entrance to the **Buffalo Bill Memorial Museum**. This surprisingly large museum (you don't really expect something this size on top of a mountain) provides a most informative look at the life and times of Buffalo Bill. It separates the man from the legend and will give you a better appreciation of him. Your visit to the park, museum and gravesite will take over an hour.

One last attraction worth mentioning is the **Mother Cabrini Shrine** located near Exit 259 off I-70. In addition to the shrine itself, there is a 22-foot statue of Christ atop a stairway of more than 370 steps! It's quite a climb and if you have any sort of physical limitation, skip it. For those who do take the almost one-hour round-trip climb (fortunately, the steps are gradual) there is a magnificent view of the entire Denver area.

DENVER ODDS AND ENDS: As befits a city of Denver's size, there is a full range of cultural and recreational activities for everyone. The **Denver Performing Arts Center** is a complex where you can watch symphony, theater, opera and more. Activity guides distributed in most hotels and available at the Visitors' Bureau can provide you with full details. Spectator sports are popular. **Mile-High Stadium**, long home to the Broncos of the National Football League, now also attracts throngs to see baseball's Denver Rockies (a nickname that really fits!). The Nuggets of the NBA play in the

McNichols Sports Arena and there is plenty in the way of college sports both in Denver and nearby Boulder.

While I seldom feel a pressing need to visit the local shopping malls, if that's your "thing" then the dozens of major malls all over the Denver area (and especially along the major highways leading out of the city) will delight you. But for more meaningful shopping, try the pedestrian-only shopping mall that runs along 16th Street downtown. There is free shuttle service if you get tired of walking between the two department stores and scores of other shops that line the 12-block-long mall. Another interesting place to shop is the Civil War-era **Larimer Square** on Larimer Street between 14th and 15th Streets. This once run-down part of town has been carefully restored and now is home to many chic shops and trendy restaurants and clubs.

You can indulge in many recreational pursuits in Denver's public parks. Hiking and climbing are available in the nearby mountains and will be described below. For those visiting in winter (or even spring and fall in many instances), there are major ski resorts within an hour's drive from Denver.

When it comes to selecting a place to stay in Denver the problem is · that the choice may be too big. Within the downtown area rates can range from $75 to more than $200 a night per couple. There are historic bed and breakfasts in the area, along with major luxury chains such as **Marriott, Hyatt Regency** and **Radisson**. There is an **Embassy Suites** hotel which may offer more suitable accommodations for families or friends traveling together. Away from downtown prices drop to between $40 and $150 per night depending upon location and degree of luxury. All of the major chains are well represented and there are dozens of independents and smaller chains. While accommodations can be found all over the Denver area, they tend to cluster along I-70 and Quebec Street near the airport, along I-25 especially near the junction of I-225, near Exit 262 off I-70, and along US 6 in the vicinity of the Denver Federal Center. The latter two of these are located west of downtown.

The selection of places to eat in a city like Denver is far beyond the scope of this book. You can find anything and everything. Consult local magazines or newspapers or ask at your hotel for suggestions.

It's now time to leave Denver and start the journey through the real Colorado – the Colorado of mountains and wilderness, of perennially snow-capped peaks and small towns. Whatever your departure point, it should be easy to work your way to I-25 northbound. Take that to Exit 217 and follow US 36, a controlled-access highway, to the attractive city of **Boulder**, a distance of about 30 miles. Originally one of many early mining settlements, Boulder has become a leading high-tech community and is home to the **University of Colorado**. US 36 ends as it reaches town and you will come upon the main campus. It is attractive and easily recognized by its Spanish-style red-brick-roofed buildings, although rapid growth has led to use of more modern styles as well. This is particularly noticable on the newer East Campus and the Williams Village campus. The **University Museum** (located in the Henderson Building on 15th Street) is an excellent natural history museum. If you missed the Denver Natural History Museum, now is your opportunity to make up for it. Allow about an hour to cover the major exhibits.

An unusual attraction is the **National Center for Atmospheric Research**. You can take a self-guiding tour (allow a minimum of 30 minutes) through displays on climate and weather, astronomy, the atmosphere and even the world of supercomputers. The famous architect I.M. Pei designed the futuristic building. NCAR is on Table Mesa Drive, in the southern part of the city.

Boulder's attraction as a place to live, study, and work has a great deal to do with its wonderful natural setting. Where else can you find a city of nearly 100,000 having a water supply that originates in a glacier? The **Arapaho Glacier**, some 30 miles distant from the city, is the water source. Boulder's recreational activities and the enjoyment of nature are enhanced by one of the largest systems of municipal parklands in the country. In the case of Boulder these are primarily mountain parks – almost 9,000 acres of which provide a setting that is hard to forget. For an introduction to these parks, take the Flagstaff Scenic Highway to the top of Flagstaff Mountain. Baseline Road provides access to Panorama Point at the top of the mountain. More than 1,600 feet beneath you lies the lovely city and to the east are the plains. Behind you, the Continental Divide's peaks soar an additional 6,000 feet above the point where you are standing – an already lofty elevation of 6,950 feet. A good network of roads traverses many sections of **Boulder Mountain Park**, with each turn providing breathtaking views as well as access to miles of trails with numerous waterfalls.

Boulder has many chain-affiliated and independent hotels and motels to select from, although the prices are generally higher than you would expect for a city of this size. It may be that there are too many people here visiting the high-tech corporations on expense accounts.

Canyon Boulevard, a main street in the center of town, becomes CO 119 as you head west out of Boulder. It climbs through the mountains and curves gently alongside **Middle Boulder Creek**. Frequent roadside pullouts make good spots to picnic or just relax and admire the surroundings. In 14 miles you'll reach CO 72 where you should turn right (northbound). This is another scenic route that leads through many small towns with fitting names, such as **Peaceful Valley**. At the town of Raymond it links up with CO 7. Continuing north, CO 7 runs parallel to the southeastern border of Rocky Mountain National Park. You won't be entering the park for quite some time yet, but the views of 13-14,000-foot mountains such as **Isolation Peak** and **Longs Peak** make this a memorable drive. The road passes very close to the **Twin Sisters Peaks** which soar a staggering 11,400 feet. This 18-mile stretch of CO 7 between Allenspark and Estes Park will have you surrounded by mountains on all sides.

The town of **Estes Park** is both a gateway to The Rocky Mountain National Park and a major resort in itself. The town, at the east end of Big Thompson Canyon (US 34), is reminiscent of towns in the Swiss Alps. A great way to combine sightseeing and recreation here is to raft the river. There are several local tour operators that specialize in river trips. However, be advised that these excursions take from a half- to a full day, so be sure you have that kind of time available. There are a number of attractions in town which depict local history and culture. Two fine examples are the **Estes Park Area Historical Museum** and the **MacGregor Ranch and Museum**. An extensive display of pewter sculptures can be found two miles east of town on US 34 at the **Michael Ricker Museum and Gallery**. Tours explain the process of casting in pewter and you can admire a 200-square-foot miniature Victorian village. Allow about 30 minutes.

An aerial tramway will take you to the top of **Prospect Mountain** and back in under a half-hour. This allows a few minutes to admire the view from the edge of town at an elevation of 8,700 feet.

If you enjoy fishing, there are a number of establishments that offer well-stocked trout ponds in pleasant settings.

There are nearly 50 motels and lodges in Estes Park. Most are unaffiliated with national chains and therefore rather expensive. **Best Western, Holiday Inn,** and **Comfort Inn** are all represented.

From Estes Park, head west for a couple of miles on US 36. This leads you to one of Colorado's highlights – **Rocky Mountain National Park**. If Colorado is the heart of the Rockies, then this park can be considered the heart of Colorado. This massive expanse of land contains more than 70 mountain peaks over 12,000 feet in elevation and even the lowest portions of the park are over 8,000 feet. There are two distinct sides to the park; one being heavily forested and the other consisting of rocky and jagged terrain with precipitous drops. The mountain peaks here are covered with snow throughout the year and, indeed, the park contains some of the largest glaciers in the lower 48 states. If the thin air didn't affect you in Denver, it might very well do so here, so it is advisable to pace yourself until you become accustomed to less oxygen.

Entering the park from US 36 will bring you directly to the **Moraine Park Visitor Center**, where rangers are available to answer any questions you may have. **Bear Lake Road** is a short spur that leads from the center to a lake of the same name. A short, flat trail (one-half mile) goes around the lake and affords some spectacular views and breathtaking scenery. The crystal clear waters reflect the surrounding mountains so perfectly that you'll feel as though you're in nature's hall of mirrors. The silence here is stunning (unless you happen to be too close to some tourists who don't appreciate the peacefulness). Once you finish this walk, drive back to the Visitor Center and pick up Trail Ridge Road.

Trail Ridge Road is the main attraction of the park. This 45-mile section of US 34 is one of the highest continuous through routes in the country and provides one spectacle after another. The road is paved and well maintained, but there are steep grades and some very sharp curves and switchbacks. Almost all of the many overlooks are located in the switchbacks themselves, where the road has been widened somewhat to allow you to stop away from traffic (remember, this is a through route so traffic, including trucks, can be heavy at times). The **Alpine Visitor Center** is located on this road at an elevation of almost 11,000 feet and the panorama from this point is unforgettable – mountains and valleys in every direction. Cars below look like insects snaking their way along the seemingly endless series of rising and falling turns.

The more adventurous may want to try a 10-mile drive on the **Fall River Road** (backtrack from the Morraine Park Visitor Center to Estes Park and take the US 34 entrance). This unpaved road is equally beautiful, but the driving far more demanding. It will give you more of a wilderness experience as well as a chance to see some of the larger cascading waterfalls. It rejoins Trail Ridge at the Fall River Pass.

At Fall River Pass the road begins to drop steadily, unlike the dramatic rise on the other side of the park. The scenery is still wonderful though not quite as eye-catching as on earlier parts of the drive. You will get a good view of several lakes including Grand, Shadow Mountain and Granby, the latter being the largest lake in the park.

Except for the Bear Lake Trail, most hikes in the park are very difficult, involving dramatic changes in elevation and rough terrain. Many people like to see the park by horseback which is an excellent option if you have the time. Otherwise, a half-day will be sufficient time to drive through, admire the views, stop at the Visitor Center and walk around Bear Lake.

Just outside the park is the town of Granby and the junction with US 40. Food and accommodations are available here. Take US 40 eastbound. If, for any reason, you thought that the scenery would end because Rocky Mountain Park is behind you, think again. The 45-mile stretch of US 40 between Granby and the junction with I-70 must rank as one of the most picturesque highways in America. Mountains and valleys surround you as you parallel the Fraser River and cross the Continental Divide at Berthoud Pass (11,314 feet). The ride might be more exciting than you expect, particularly if you haven't been exposed to mountain driving before. The drop is steep so go slow and use low gear. Upon reaching I-70 (and breathing a sigh of relief!) head west four miles to the town of Georgetown (Exit 228).

Georgetown is a page right out of history – in this case, gold rush history circa 1859. At one time this town, dubbed "Silver Queen," was the largest in Colorado. The current population is under a thousand, but the town retains over 200 buildings from its heyday, most of which have been converted to shops that accommodate tourists hungry to buy almost anything. Two buildings that remain relatively untouched are the **Hamill House** and the **Hotel de Paris**. Both structures exemplify the wealth that Georgetown once possessed. The hotel also houses a museum that details the rise and fall of this mining town, typical of so many throughout the state. Allow about an hour to tour both sites.

If you want to spend more time in the Georgetown area, take a ride on the authentic steam-powered **Georgetown Loop Historic Mining Area Train**. Built in the roaring 20s, the train follows a route through the surrounding silver mining country. The ride takes 2 1/2 hours and includes a tour through an old mine. Georgetown is tiny but still offers lodging and quite a few places to eat.

Now it's back onto I-70, continuing in a westerly direction. This is a wide interstate highway so you don't have to worry about difficult driving conditions. If you rented a car in Denver it should already be adjusted for high altitude driving. Those coming in their own vehicles should make the necessary adjustments for better performance in rarified air. At Milepost 212 the highway starts to cut through the mountains instead of going over or around them. **The Eisenhower Tunnel** is one of the longest such tunnels in the United States and is quite an engineering achievement. It passes beneath the Continental Divide. Several towns along this portion of the highway offer lodging. One of the nicest, both in terms of facilities and location, is the magnificent **Keystone Resort** (Exit 205). You'll also encounter an enormous selection of places to stay at our next stop, the town of Vail. Use Exit 176 for direct access into Vail.

Vail is Colorado's most famous winter resort. It was built to resemble an Alpine vacationland and the Swiss motif is apparent to every visitor both in the names of establishments and the architectural style. This quaint town deserves its reputation as a world class resort and, although you won't be skiing in summer, there are many other activities here. Musical entertainment is presented throughout the summer months and several operators run rafting trips on the Colorado River. Information on these and other activities is available at either of two Visitor Centers (located at each end of the town) or at the Tourism and Convention Bureau.

The **Vail Ski Area** can be visited in summer since one of the gondolas used to transport winter ski bunnies is converted to a tourist toter. There are more than 11 square miles of skiing routes on this single mountain, making it one of the largest such facilities in the nation. Regardless of your passion for snow, you should find time to visit the **Colorado Ski Museum and Hall of Fame**, located two blocks from the Interstate. The history of skiing is documented and its heroes are honored. Allow a half-hour for this visit. **Vail Village** is a pedestrian town so most cars must be left at one of the large garages or parking lots at the end of town. Strolling through the town is a very pleasant way to spend an hour or so. A small amphitheater in the village contains the **Betty Ford Alpine Gardens** that offer ponds and man-made waterfalls and reveal beautiful blossoms in the summer.

Accommodations in Vail are varied, but very high-priced. Several chains and an interesting assortment of independent hotels are here. Dining covers the international spectrum and tends to be on the ritzy and expensive side too, but for lunch you can find plenty of sandwich shops and other places that won't bust the budget.

From Vail take I-70 another five miles west to Exit 171, then travel south on US 24 for 32 miles. This stretch of US 24 passes through some national forests and once again over the Continental Divide at the Tennessee Pass. Your destination for now is the town of **Leadville**. As the name implies, lead and other minerals are found here, but it wasn't always that way. The site was originally called Oro City and was founded during the 1860 gold rush. However, so little of the precious metal was found that the boom town quickly died, but it has produced a fortune in valuable minerals. It once had a population of over 30,000, that figure is now less than 3,000. At an altitude of over 10,000 feet, Leadville lays claim to being the highest incorporated city in the United States.

Harrison Avenue is the main street in town and is scattered with attractions. The **Earth Runs Silver** is an excellent 30-minute multimedia presentation on the town's turbulent history. The **Heritage Museum** also documents Leadville lore with artifacts and exhibits. Like all mining communities, Leadville has its share of opulent homes built by those who struck it rich. Harrison Avenue's **Healy House** is one of the better examples of the genre with costumed guides giving tours. While it looks quite ordinary from the outside, the interior is richly paneled and decorated. Allow 30-45 minutes for exploring the Healy complex.

Among other attractions in town are the **Tabor House** and **Tabor Opera House**. Mr. Tabor was one of Leadville's wealthiest citizens (although he stuck with a particular claim too long and died in poverty). His home is furnished as it was in the late 1880s. The Opera House allows you to take a self-guiding tour. Famous stars of the day were invited to perform here and the building has been restored to its appearance when the last show was staged.

Although you may have had your fill of museums devoted to mining, you should make time for one more – the **National Mining Hall of Fame and Museum**. This one doesn't just trace the history of mining in Colorado, it explores the industry as far back as the ancient Egyptians and is one of the most comprehensive museums of its type to be found. Allow at least 30 minutes.

Like Georgetown, Leadville has an historic train ride. If you didn't take the one in Georgetown, you might be interested in the 2 1/2-hour trip with the **Leadville, Colorado and Southern Railroad Company**. If you feel that "seeing one is seeing them all," then pick one town and skim through the others. If you opt to tour only one in detail, Leadville is an excellent choice. This town has several motels if you choose to spend the night in town.

We'll now continue on US 24 for another 15 miles. This ride provides an excellent view of 14,433-foot Mt. Elbert, Colorado's loftiest peak. It is beautiful, but the difference in height between it and dozens of others is not readily apparent. In fact, many other peaks will appear to be higher because they rise more sharply from the surrounding terrain. Turn right on CO 82 and enjoy the 44 miles to our next stop, Aspen. Along the way you'll be crossing the Continental Divide two more times. Views at Independence Pass are worth a special mention.

Aspen was once a mining community but there is little evidence of that now. It has been turned into a year-round resort that can compete with Vail with its facilities and beauty. The summer season brings the **American Music Festival**, which draws both aspiring and accomplished artists and crowds of listeners. There is a dance festival as well. The recreational opportunities within this area are endless. Among these are backcountry jeep trips, horseback riding, hiking, bike trips and river rafting. Tour operators are easy to find, but it is wiser to consult the helpful staff at one of Aspen's two Visitor Centers, the most convenient one being at the

Rio Grande Parking Plaza (that's where most visitors leave their cars when exploring the town).

While a stroll through town offers a combination of historic and modern buildings and shops, the best attractions are outside of town. There are a number of very interesting ghost towns in the vicinity, the easiest one to reach being **Independence Ghost Town**. This is 15 miles before town on CO 82 so you can stop on the way into town if you want to avoid the extra mileage back and forth. The town has been abandoned for over 90 years now and it looks it. Feel free to walk around but do not attempt to enter any of the buildings. There is always the danger of a possible collapse. This is not a restoration – the buildings have been left as they were.

Perhaps Aspen is most famous for the **Maroon Bells**, pyramid-shaped mountains of such symmetry and graceful beauty that they are said to be the most photographed peaks in all of Colorado. I don't know if the claim is true, but they are a sight that should not be missed. The 10-mile road to them is restricted to overnight campers, but a round-trip bus service is provided from town at frequent intervals. Aside from its beauty, Maroon Bells offers an attractive lake and plenty of opportunities for walking and hiking. Approximately 90 minutes should be allotted to this excursion.

There are plenty of accommodations in Aspen and the neighboring resort community of Snowmass. As in Vail, they are very high-priced.

Continue on CO 82 when you leave Aspen. It is 42 miles back to the junction of I-70 at the town of **Glenwood Springs**. Here you can take a dip (for a fee) in a natural hot springs pool. An 18-mile stretch of Glenwood Canyon lies east of town along I-70. This is out of the way but is worth the trip, especially if you are willing to hike the fairly strenuous trail (nearly two miles) to **Bridal Veil Falls** and **Hanging Lake**. The falls are beautiful but Hanging Lake is unique – the lake is on a cliff more than 1,200 feet above the canyon floor and appears to be suspended above it. The trail head is located 10 miles east of Glenwood Springs. Unless you are physically handicapped the trail shouldn't present a problem. If you take this side trip allow between two and three hours including the round-trip on I-70. There is a wide choice of lodging in Glenwood Springs, including **Best Western, Holiday Inn** and **Ramada** hotels.

Heading west once again on I-70, it is 85 miles from Glenwood Springs to Grand Junction (use Exit 31 for access into town). The ride is quick since the Interstate presents no unusual driving conditions. I-70 parallels the Colorado River and there are mountains on either side of you. While the scenery is lovely along this portion of the road it doesn't match the spectacular sights that you will have encountered since leaving Denver. Be assured that there will be plenty of great scenery ahead!

With a population of nearly 30,000, **Grand Junction** is the largest community in the sparsely populated west-central portion of the state. The attractions here are all out of town and we'll discuss them in a moment. It is a sensible place to base yourself for an evening as there is a good selection of reasonably priced accommodations, including many chain motels. The main thing that brings tourists to Grand Junction is the nearby **Colorado National Monument**. While it may not be famous compared to many other National Park Service areas, anyone who visits will be deeply impressed by its gigantic and colorful formations, the products of erosion over many eons. You can reach the monument from the center of town (follow signs) or by Exit 19 off I-70 west of town. You can take either route because the 23-mile **Rim Rock Drive** that traverses Colorado National Monument connects the entrance stations at either end.

The two-way road is well paved and easy to drive. Most of the route is at the top of the formation (as suggested by the road's name) and you look down on the sights. The rise in elevation is accomplished by a series of switchbacks (including some tunnels at the western end) that will bring you up almost 1,000 feet from the valley. All of the worthwhile sights within the monument can be seen from roadside pullouts or by very short walks. For those who have the time, energy and perhaps the courage, there is an extensive system of trails allowing you to climb down and touch some of the fantastic formations. You should stop at the Visitor Center to acquaint yourself with the geology of the area. Among the better view stops are Redlands View, Balanced Rock, Distant View, Independence View, Grand View, Monument Canyon View, Artist Point and Highland View. Short trails that everyone can and should do are the ones to **Window Rock, Canyon Rim Trail** and the **Coke Ovens Trail**. Throughout the Monument you will see red sandstone rocks of every imaginable shape, sometimes rising to heights of 1,000 feet. The Coke Ovens are well named – their shape makes them appear almost to have been put there by the hand of man. Including the time to drive the rim road, stop at many of the viewing areas and take the three short trails mentioned, a visit to Colorado National Monument will take about 2 1/2 to 3 hours. Allow longer if you are going to be attempting any of the other trails.

Upon leaving the monument or Grand Junction pick up US 50 heading east. There are some outstanding roadside sights along this route. They will be covered in the Alternative Routes section of this chapter since they add a significant amount of mileage and can be difficult to get to. Just over 40 miles from Grand Junction, US 50 will bring you to the town of Delta. A good way to break up the ride to the next major destination is by stopping here to visit **Fort Uncompahgre**, a former fur trading post that was built in the 1820s. The fort has been restored and costumed personnel carry out daily activities typical of those that were done more than 150 years ago. Tours are available or you can walk around on your own. One hour will be sufficient for visiting Fort Uncompahgre.

From Delta it is another 21 miles on US 50 to Montrose. Stay on US 50 for another eight miles until you reach CO 347, take this road for six miles to the spectacular **Black Canyon of the Gunnison National Monument**. When nature is at its best words are never adequate to describe what you will see. The Black Canyon is such a place. This is not a huge canyon when compared to the Grand Canyon or even the Colorado National Monument's canyons. But it is unique in its combination of depth, narrowness and sheer drops. The canyon is 12 miles long and almost 2,700 feet deep with a width that barely approaches 1,200 feet in some places. Portions of the bottom are only 40 feet wide! The precipitous canyon walls keep out sunlight, hence the name. The dark color of the rock is another reason for the canyon's name. Barely visible at the bottom as you peer down is the Gunnison River. After a brief stop at the Visitor Center take the three mile road that runs along the rim. Overlooks are either right on the road or can be reached by a short walk. The main viewing areas are Gunnison Point, Chasm View, Sunset View and High Point. The only longer trail (unless you are a very experienced climber and wish to descend into the canyon, an arduous journey) is the 1 1/2-mile Warren Point Trail at the end of the road. The trail is easy and leads to another breathtaking view of the canyon.

There is also a north rim that can be visited, but it requires considerable extra mileage, some of which is on more difficult roads and the view is not substantially different. Therefore, the Black Canyon can take under an hour to visit, unless you do the Warren Point Trail. In that case you should plan on spending about 1 3/4 hours there.

After leaving Black Canyon (if you can tear yourself away) go back to Montrose, turning right towards town at the junction of US 550. Among several in-town motels are a **Best Western** and **Days Inn**. Four miles south of town is the **Ute Indian Museum**, a fascinating exhibit on the Ute Indians and the Spanish missionaries they assisted in exploring and mapping the area. Your explorations should take under a half-hour.

Another 32 miles on US 550 through pleasant scenery will bring you to the town of Ouray, named for a former Ute Indian chieftain. Anyone who is planning to get into the backcountry for some four-wheel-drive tours can arrange such a trip here. The San Juan Mountains provide an excellent place to explore the wilderness. A mile north of town off of US 550 (follow signs) is the **Bachelor-Syracuse Mine**. Originally settled to mine for silver, Ouray was successful in that endeavor as well as in gold mining. The mine produced millions of dollars worth of each ore. You can take an hour-long guided tour on a mine train, traveling over half a mile into Gold Hill Mountain to see how mining operations were done. Bring along a sweater or light jacket since the interior of the mine is a chilly 50 degrees.

Within the town itself is the incredible **Box Canyon**, with a width of only 20 feet and a height of about 220. The canyon does look like a large box when viewed from a bridge which spans the gorge. There is also a trail to a beautiful waterfall that feeds the creek running through Box Canyon. You can complete a visit to the canyon in 30 minutes.

An adventure awaits you upon departing from Ouray, for you are about to embark on the **Million Dollar Highway**. Although it refers to a particularly scenic six-mile stretch of the road, the name is often used for the entire 23-mile distance between Ouray and Silverton. The name comes from the value of the ore that was once mined in the area, although many people think it is named for the scenery. The views are priceless. Be careful as you drive along the narrow and mountainous road. Sometimes the canyon the road passes through is so narrow that all you can see above is a towering wall. At other times it offers spectacular views, such as the one of lofty Mt. Abrams. Another highlight along the Million Dollar Highway is **Bear Creek Falls**, where the cascade plunges nearly 230 feet into the canyon below. You will find many parking areas scattered along US 550 so you can get out and admire the scenery without endangering yourself or other motorists.

For now we'll pass through the town of Silverton without mentioning any details, because our suggested route will soon have you returning to this point via train. However, if you do not plan to take the famous narrow gauge railway from Durango to Silverton, you might want to turn to the information on Silverton.

It is another 50 miles along US 550 from Silverton to Durango with the scenery still highly rewarding (perhaps this should be called the Half-Million Dollar Highway) as you cruise along near the Animas River through the San Juan Mountains. Much of the route parallels the railroad and offers a different type of scenery. If you opt to take the Durango/Silverton train you will find the views far superior to those from the road. One stop that should be made is at **Lime Creek Canyon**, where you will see a small but very deep (2,000 feet) canyon.

Durango is an interesting little town with lots of activity. There's plenty of shopping for the droves of visitors who come here and a huge selection of hotels. Many major chains are represented, including a well known western chain called **Red Lion**, but two historic hotels might be of special interest to you. These are the **General Palmer** and, especially, the **Strater Hotel**. The latter is a Victorian structure that, despite having modern conveniences, will make you feel that you are back around the turn of the century. An interesting nightly attraction at the hotel is the **Diamond Circle Melodrama**, a combination of Victorian melodrama and vaudeville. The choice of where to eat in Durango is as wide as for lodging. A very popular choice for dinner is the **Bar D Chuckwagon**, which combines a single seating cowboy-style dinner for hundreds, including seconds, with a zany and entertaining revue suitable for children and adults.

Durango's real claim to fame is as the departure point for the wonderful all-day excursion on the **Durango & Silverton Narrow Gauge Railroad**. Real mining locomotives pull hundreds of visitors in two morning departures. Some of the passenger cars are open air, but even those traveling in the enclosed cars will probably find themselves covered with soot from the locomotives. Wear dark clothes and sit towards the back where the ash is far less pronounced. It's great fun as you imagine yourself taking a trip into town after working the mines. The scenery is gorgeous – consisting of the rushing Animas River and both near and distant mountains, many covered with snow. The train stops for about two hours in Silverton which is more than enough time to have lunch in one of the many restaurants and to walk around this town that time forgot. Silverton has a population of about 700 people, which is less than the amount of tourists who come there each day by train. The streets are wooden boardwalks and the whole place looks as it did a hundred years ago. But this is not a restoration – this is, as they say, the real thing!

Be sure to make reservations for the train well in advance as it is an exceedingly popular attraction that fills up early. Call (303) 247-2733 or write to the **Ticket Office**, 479 Main Ave., Durango CO 81301.

From Durango take US 160 in a westerly direction for 36 miles to the entrance of **Mesa Verde National Park**. This will likely be one of the highlights of your Colorado journey. Rare is the case where a National Park provides both outstanding scenery and history, but Mesa Verde is such a place. The name means "Green Table" and it is, indeed, a large and nearly flat-topped, heavily forested plateau 2,000 feet above the surrounding landscape. An ancient Indian culture lived on Mesa Verde as far back as 500 A.D. The current ruins, which comprise one of the country's most significant archaeological sites, date mostly from the 13th century. Most of the dwellings were built into crevices beneath the cliff top – their location designed to provide protection. A visit here will give you a good understanding of how these people lived, while allowing you to see some of southwestern Colorado's finest scenery.

The road climbs for about 20 miles from the park's entrance to the top of the mesa. Along the way you'll encounter increasingly sharp turns before entering a long tunnel. After emerging from the tunnel the road rises even more dramatically in a series of switchbacks. Two places that you can stop to admire the magnificent panorama are at the Montezuma Valley Overlook and Park Point, the latter being reached via a short spur road. Soon after reaching the top make a stop at the **Far View Visitor Center**. This large and modern building has an excellent museum that provides a comprehensive explanation of the Indian cultures that made Mesa Verde their home. Far View also is the site of a nice motor lodge, the **Far View**

Inn, for those wishing to stay in the park. Several restaurants are here as well.

After Far View the park road splits into two loops which are easy to follow and provide access to the major sights. Cliff dwellings such as **Spruce Tree Ruin, Square Tower House, Sun Point** (for a view of Mesa Verde's most important ruin – **Cliff House**) and dozens of smaller structures, can be viewed from the road or reached by short walks. If you only have time to go inside one of the dwellings, then Spruce Tree is the best choice. Cliff House and **Balcony House,** another impressive ruin, can also be visited, but they are not as easy to reach because both require climbing steep ladders.

A final option when touring Mesa Verde is to take the side road from just past Far View that leads to the adjacent **Wetherill Mesa.** There are more cliff dwellings here and it has the advantage of being far less crowded. On the other hand, the road is somewhat more difficult. Allow between three and four hours for visiting Mesa Verde – longer if you will be going to Wetherill.

When you return to US 160 after leaving Mesa Verde, our suggested route heads back east towards Durango. However, if it is late in the day and you're looking for a place to bed down for the night but don't want to stay in the Park, you can go 10 miles west on US 160 to the town of Cortez. This town offers a variety of reasonably priced lodgings. Summer visitors who happen to be here between Monday and Thursday will have the chance to watch the colorful evening performance of Indian dancers in City Park.

The distance between Durango and the next group of major attractions in Canon City is about 240 miles, the longest ride of the entire main itinerary. (An alternative route is discussed later.) But you won't be doing it in one fell swoop since there are several minor attractions along the way to break things up. The first of these is a splendid view of **Chimney Rock,** about 40 miles east of Durango and seen from S 160. This is a high mesa that rises prominently and dramatically from the surprisingly flat tablelands. Shortly after Chimney Rock is the town of **Pagosa Springs** which, although it doesn't have much to see, is a possible place for lodging and dining. Between Pagosa Springs and Del Norte, US 160 crosses the Continental Divide at **Wolf Creek Pass** (elevation 10,550 feet). From here there are dramatic views of large portions of the mountainous San Juan and Rio Grande National Forests. In fact, the

44-mile section from Pagosa Springs to just before Del Norte is very scenic and is the best part of the ride to Canon City.

Del Norte is home to the **Rio Grande County Museum**, which has exhibits on regional natural and cultural history. Upon leaving Del Norte, you'll also leave US 160 and take CO 112 for 13 miles to the junction of US 285. Turn left and follow this road north for just over 60 miles to the junction of US 50. Five miles east on US 50 is the town of **Salida**. If you want to try a backcountry wilderness tour, this is the place. Salida also has many hotels and restaurants. For those who have never visited a fish hatchery the **Mt. Shavano State Fish Hatchery** (one mile from town on CO 291) is a worthwhile stop. It is interesting to see how different kinds of trout by the millions are raised on this 25-acre site. These hatcheries help to keep lakes and streams adequately stocked for fishermen.

Now you've reached the final stretch to **Canon City**, which is only 47 more miles on US 50. The town doesn't have too many motels but there is a **Best Western** and a **Days Inn** and several good restaurants. As you will find throughout Colorado, steak houses are very popular. We've jumped ahead a little here because the attractions of Canon City are mainly eight miles before town where the gorge of the Arkansas River and the surrounding mountains provide plenty of beautiful sights. These attractions have not been made part of national or state parks, but are all commercial enterprises. Despite some tacky additions, nature is still the main attraction and you'll be rewarded for the time spent here. Whitewater rafting is a popular activity in this area.

The two most important sightseeing stops for visitors are **Buckskin Joe** and the **Royal Gorge Bridge**. Buckskin Joe is a large (160-acre) mining town where you can pan for gold like a prospector, take a ride on a stagecoach or horse, see a mock gun fight, or look at vintage cars and trains. There are also numerous other activities for children. To the author, however, the highlight of Buckskin Joe is the three-mile ride on the miniature railway to the edge of the mighty **Royal Gorge**. Even better views of the gorge are at the Royal Gorge Bridge, a private park. The suspension bridge across this geologic wonder is the highest in the world, connecting the two rims of the canyon at a height of 1,053 feet above the Arkansas River. The bridge is narrow and can only be crossed by cars. Campers and other large vehicles must park at the end of the bridge and their occupants can either walk across or take the trolley service. You can get to the bottom of the narrow and deep canyon by taking an incline railway, or you can cross over it on an aerial tramway. While this doesn't provide a view much different than the one from the bridge, the experience is a lot more exciting! The area also contains scenic trails for short or long walks and attractions that will appeal to the kids. Allow a minimum of 90 minutes for the Royal Gorge Bridge, while Buckskin Joe should take up about an hour of your time unless you extend it by taking some of the rides.

Skyline Drive is four miles closer to town and is a three-mile one-way road that will carry you across the top of a ridge that rises about 800 feet above the town of Canon City. The road is narrow but not unusually difficult.

From the town of Canon City you'll continue on US 50 eastbound for 11 more miles and take CO 115 north into Colorado's second largest city and, in some ways, first city of attractions – **Colorado Springs**. This fast growing metropolis now has a population of over 280,000, with the metropolitan area approaching 400,000. At the foot of Pikes Peak, one could not ask for a much better location. Its setting means there are many outdoor attractions in addition to those normally associated with a city. You can get the best of both worlds in Colorado Springs. I-25 is the main north-south artery in the city, while US 24 provides the primary means of east-west travel (like the Midland Expressway on the west side of town, and Platte Avenue in the east). Things are rather spread out, so you'll have to get around by car. Unfortunately, there isn't much of a street pattern here so we'll divide the many attractions into four different areas to avoid confusion. Touring in the sections will enable you to avoid piling up extra miles running here and there with no logical order. This will apply even if you don't do everything in a given area. The four segments are (a) East of I-25, (b) the Southwest & Broadmoor area, (c) the neighboring community of Manitou Springs which is immediately to the west of Colorado Springs, and (d) Northwest. The last three are all west of I-25, also known as the Monument Valley Freeway. Other attractions in the vicinity of Colorado Springs will be found in the Alternative Routes section of this chapter.

EAST: Our first attraction is **Peterson Air and Space Museum**, four miles east of downtown via US 24 (Platte Avenue). Besides the usual exhibits on historic aircraft, especially as they relate to Colorado Springs, the museum has many interesting features on the North American Air Defense Command (NORAD). The headquarters of that organization is buried in one of the mountains that form the city's western edge. Allow 45 minutes minimum and longer if you wish to view the many films that are showing.

Head back on US 24 for about three miles to Union Blvd. Take that to E. Boulder Street, turn left and proceed until you reach the **U.S. Olympic Complex**. Besides being the headquarters of our country's Olympic Committee, the site houses complete training facilities for aspiring Olympic athletes. Informative one-hour guided tours of the nearly 40-acre complex are given. About a mile to the east at 818 N.Cascade Avenue is the **Museum of the American Numismatic Association**. The many beautiful galleries here display an enormous collection of both coin and paper currency along with medals from ancient times right up to the present day. Even if you are not a coin collector this is a fascinating museum where you can pass a quick and informative hour.

SOUTHWEST & BROADMOOR: This is the scenic portion of the city, tucked into the foothills of the Rockies. It is also the home of most of Colorado Springs' many fabulous vacation and resort complexes. Exit 138 of I-25 will provide a quick means of access to the area via Lake Avenue. On this street is the **El Pomar Carriage House Museum**, showing a range of early non-motorized vehicles. These include a Conestoga wagon and coaches that were used in Presidential inaugurations. Saddles and related equipment round out the fine collection. It can be seen in 30-45 minutes. The museum is in front of one of the world's most famous and elegant resort hotels – **The Broadmoor**. Dating from 1918, this large hotel is at the foot of beautiful Cheyenne Mountain. The enormous grounds are meticulously kept and worth a visit even if you are not going to be staying here – which is likely considering the $200-$300 nightly rate! Ah, to be rich and think nothing of checking in to a place like this! At least you can get a feel for how the other half lives even if just for a short time before returning to reality.

From the Broadmoor it is just a few blocks to the **World Figure Skating Museum Hall of Fame**. The museum portion displays skating equipment and awards and has exhibits dealing with skating techniques and the sport in general. The Hall of Fame section honors outstanding skaters from around the world and you'll recognize names such as Peggy Fleming and Sonja Henie. It should take you 30 minutes to view the exhibits and hall areas.

South of the skating museum you'll run into Mirada Road. Turn left and take this street for a mile to Cheyenne Mountain Zoo Road. Another left will soon bring you to – surprise – **Cheyenne Mountain Zoo**. Hundreds of animals are kept here, primarily those native to North America. The spacious grounds are on the very slopes of Cheyenne Mountain which instills a sense of being out in the wild with nature. Time allotments for this type of attraction are difficult because some people can get very involved, but allow at least two hours. When you leave the zoo continue on the Zoo Road for two more miles to the **Shrine of the Sun**. This impressive stone monument to Will Rogers stands 8,000 feet above sea level. Facing eastward, it offers an inspiring panorama of the Colorado Springs area; to the west are the even higher mountains of the Pike National Forest. The life of Will Rogers is documented here, something that shouldn't be overlooked as you try to tear yourself away from the view. While the shrine and view won't take that long for most visitors, you might want to allow yourself some extra time to walk around this beautiful area. Note that past the zoo the route is a toll road.

Now it's time to head back down the twisting road that becomes El Pomar Road. Take that road to Cheyenne Blvd. and make a left turn. This is another winding route that traverses a huge parkland called **North Cheyenne Park**, thousands of acres covering a large portion of this part of Colorado Springs. Cheyenne Blvd. will take you into **North Cheyenne Canyon** and beyond to **High Drive**. The canyon is absolutely beautiful and is highlighted by unusual rock formations and several waterfalls. The **Silver Cascades** are especially breathtaking. It will take you 30-45 minutes to explore North Cheyenne Canyon. High Drive provides even more spectacular scenery along its 10-mile route, which begins where Cheyenne Canyon Boulevard ends. Although the rewards are great, it must be emphasized that High Drive is only for experienced mountain drivers. Besides being extremely steep, the road has no guard rails for physical or psychological protection. If you feel up to it, allow at least an hour because slow is the only acceptable pace along here.

Now head back towards town until you reach the intersection of North Cheyenne and Cheyenne Canyon Boulevards. There is another road that branches off here and leads several miles to the **Seven Falls**, so named because they form tiers. The sight of them cascading into the deep canyon will leave a lasting impression. There is an excellent vantage point – Eagle's Nest – from which to view the falls. Early visitors had to climb over 200 steps to get to it (which you can still do if you're ambitious), but most people now take the more convenient elevator. The falls are illuminated at night during the summer season. If you intend to see this very dramatic sight, come specifically for that purpose from town and head directly back. Don't attempt to drive through North Cheyenne Canyon at night. The falls are in a park setting, with many trails, so consider spending an hour or so here to take in the tranquil surroundings.

MANITOU SPRINGS: This town can be reached by the Midland Expressway (US 24) west from downtown or I-25 Exit 141. All of the attractions in Manitou Springs are located near the Expressway. In fact, the first point of interest is right on the US 24 bypass that runs alongside the main road. **Manitou Cliff Dwellings Museum** documents the culture of Indian civilizations in the Southwest during the era when the greatest pueblos were built. This was approximately 800 years ago. A lot of emphasis is placed on the significant architectural accomplishments that were achieved. An added attraction during the summer is the performance of Indian dances by native Americans. Allow about an hour for your visit.

Only a half-mile further along US 24 from the Cliff Dwellings Museum will bring you to a short side road that quickly winds its way up to **Cave of the Winds**. Two separate tours are offered. Most visitors will take the 45-minute Discovery Tour, which explores about 20 different "rooms" along a well-lighted paved path covering less than a mile. A much more difficult 2 1/2-hour trip called the Wild Tour begins where the Discovery Tour leaves off. This trip is definitely for the more experienced cave visitor and children under 12 are not allowed to participate. An evening trip to the Cave of the Winds allows you to see the fabulous laser light show that is projected onto the walls of Williams Canyon. The show starts each night at 9 (summer season) and lasts about 45 minutes. Separate admission is charged for the laser show.

Manitou Avenue is a loop on the south side of the Midland Expressway. Here you will find the **Buffalo Bill Wax Museum** which houses a realistic collection of more than 30 prominent figures from the history of the American West.

Branching off Manitou Avenue is Ruxton St. Take that to the end and you'll come to what most people think of when they hear Colorado Springs (even though it is in Manitou Springs) – namely,

Pikes Peak and the **Pikes Peak Cog Railway**. This is an exciting and beautiful trip lasting 3 1/2 hours that will take you to the 14,110-foot summit. This is almost 8,000 feet higher than the base station and you can expect a drop in temperature approaching 25 degrees; bring along some warm clothing. Hopefully it will be a clear day and you'll be able to see as far as Denver or all the way into New Mexico. Such days are common here in the summer when most rain occurs as late afternoon showers. The view is fabulous no matter which direction you look, "on top of the world looking down on creation."

While most visitors to the Colorado Springs area consider Pikes Peak a must, you may feel that the trip takes too long. If so, you can take a toll road leading to the summit of **Mt. Manitou**. This is not for the timid as it is mostly unpaved with hairpin turns and steep grades. It doesn't go as high and you can't proudly proclaim to your friends that you climbed Pikes Peak but the views are also splendid and it takes only a third of the time.

NORTHWEST: Return now to Colorado Springs proper via the Midland Expressway, exiting at 21st Street and heading south for less than a mile to the **Hall of Presidents Wax Museum**. The name is misleading because the wax figures also depict persons other than American Presidents. In all there are almost 140 figures and a children's fairyland. The quality of the figures is excellent, as they are products of the famous Josephine Tussaud. There is a lot to see so plan on spending close to an hour here.

Now head back on US 24 following signs for the **Garden of the Gods**. This remarkable park is filled with fantastic sandstone formations and would seem to fit better in Utah than Colorado. Narrow roads wind through the 1,300-plus-acre park, but there are no steep grades and no driving at the edge of a mountain! The dominant color of the rocks is red but the color changes depending upon the time of day and angle of view. There is also a Visitor Center that contains the **Camera Obscura**, a periscope-like device affording a 360-degree panorama of the surrounding area. The view from outside is also wonderful, with Pikes Peak forming a backdrop. Your enjoyment will be enhanced by the fanciful names that have been given to the many formations. Although the road provides access to most of the better formations, you should get out of the car now and then to explore some of the trails. A proper visit requires about 1 1/4 hours.

If you entered the Garden of the Gods as suggested, you will exit at the northeastern gateway onto 30th Street. Turn left and travel two miles to the Garden of the Gods Road. A right turn here will bring you to I-25. Go north one exit (147) to our last suggested attraction in this section and the city, the **Pro Rodeo Hall of Fame**. Here the history, color, pageantry and excitement of rodeo comes alive through imaginative exhibits and multimedia presentations. The Hall of Champions pays tribute to outstanding figures in American rodeo. It seems that today people can find reason to object to just about anything and that includes rodeo. But rodeo is an important part of the tradition of the American West and thus this attraction should likewise be a part of your visit.

COLORADO SPRINGS ODDS AND ENDS: Participant sports of every variety can be enjoyed in Colorado Springs' numerous parks. Cultural activities are concentrated in the **Fine Arts Center**. The summer brings with it an opera festival at the **Pikes Peak Center**, the home of the Colorado Symphony. Both facilities are downtown adjacent to I-25.

In addition to the ubiquitous shopping malls, you might consider spending some time in the **Old Colorado City Historic District** between 24th and 27th Streets. Dozens of specialty shops line the area along with many restaurants. Speaking of dining, we have a soft spot for western Bar-B-Ques when in Colorado so the **Flying W Ranch Chuckwagon Suppers** is one of our favorites.

Lodging is no problem as there are dozens of hotels and motels to select from including almost every major chain with every price available (usually lower than in Denver). Accommodations are located mainly along the I-25 corridor, especially to the north and in the US 24-Midland Expressway corridor.

It is under 70 miles from Colorado Springs back to Denver, all via I-25. But you have one more stop on the way. Just north of Colorado Springs is the most beautiful of all of America's military service academies – the **United States Air Force Academy**. Use Exit 150 from I-25 then follow Southgate Drive and Pine Drive to Academy Drive and the Visitor Center. Here you can get a map of the Academy and current information as to what can be visited. Within the Center is a model of a typical cadet quarters. As the newest of the academies the architecture is modern, even futuristic looking in some cases. Set against the Rockies, it is a most dramatic sight. The Academy provides several overlooks where you can see not only the mountains, but the various building complexes. Of particular interest are the stadium, a display of aircraft and the Cadet Chapel – the most famous structure on campus. This inverted V-shaped building features stained glass windows. When viewed from above it seems about ready to take off into the wild blue yonder, and what could be more appropriate for a chapel at the Air Force Academy!

Unfortunately, cadet formations are only held during the academic year (at noon) so anyone traveling out of that time span will not see this glorious display. But there is enough to see without that and you should allow a minimum of 90 minutes for a proper self-guiding tour of this huge campus.

Arriving back in the Denver vicinity, use Exit 200 from I-25 if you are heading to the airport. This is I-225 and it will take you directly into I-70. Go west three exits (#278) to the airport. For those of our readers who joined the route elsewhere and will be continuing with their travels, stay on I-25 into the heart of downtown (Exit 210) and pick up the itinerary from the beginning of this chapter.

Alternative Routes

The suggested itinerary we've just completed covers nearly all of Colorado's major attractions and then some. However, you may have a lot of time and want to do more, or simply prefer to follow another route. That's what will be explored here. If the main itinerary is too long, then some of the following can replace portions of the previously suggested route. The first two alternatives cover areas in the vicinity of Denver while the third is a loop from Colorado Springs. The remainder are either fairly short side trips off of the main route or itineraries that replace segments of the main route.

A SHORT LOOP NORTH OF DENVER: This trip covers a total of 160 miles from downtown Denver and back and can be done in one day. Most of the sights are historic rather than scenic. However, as it all falls within a narrow corridor due north of Denver, the Rockies are always visible to the west.

Leaving Denver via I-25, it is under 50 miles to the town of Loveland, a short distance west of Exit 257. This town becomes famous each February when thousands of people mail valentines from here to their loved ones. To the west of town lies the beginning of the Big Thompson Canyon which ends at Estes Park. Within town is the **Loveland Museum**. Another of many local history museums, the most noted feature is its large topographic map of the Big Thompson Reclamation Project. It's a short but mildly interesting stop. Leave town by taking US 287 north for 10 miles to **Fort Collins**, one of the larger cities in Colorado with a population of nearly 90,000. The town dates from the Civil War era and the center of downtown has been restored and converted to an attractive area of shops. On Busch Drive is the **Anheuser-Busch Brewery**. Besides the usual tour of the brewing process and free samples in the hospitality center, visitors can tour the stables where one of the company's teams of famous Clydesdale horses are housed. Unless they're on tour somewhere you'll be able to get a close look at these beautiful animals. Saddles and other equipment used in Clydesdale promotional activities will be on display even if the team is away. Allow about an hour for your visit. The **Fort Collins Museum** documents the history of the northern portion of Colorado, from the first settlers to modern times. Local geology and agriculture are also explored at this museum, reached by taking CO 14 to Mulberry Street westbound, then turning right off Mulberry.

Retrace the few blocks back to CO 14 because you'll now be taking that road in an easterly direction for 13 miles to US 85 where you should turn south and drive for 11 miles to Greeley. In case you're thinking back to your folk history and remember that Horace Greeley said "Go west, young man," you're correct – the town was named for good old Horace, as many people who followed his call wound up settling in this area. Besides some houses from that era, the main attraction is **Historic Centennial Village**. This large restoration of a frontier village includes many examples of homes and shops, a school and church, as well as a ranch. Spanish-style adobe architecture is also on display. You can walk around the grounds and explore the buildings on your own or you may want to take a guided tour. In either case it will take an hour or more to see the entire village.

Continue south on US 85 for 16 miles to the small town of Platteville, site of **Fort Vasquez**. The fort is a complete replica of a fur trading post that was originally built around 1830. There is also a museum with interesting dioramas and exhibits that portray activities during the fort's active days. From Platteville, US 85 leads directly back into Denver, a distance of 31 miles.

behind St. Mary's Lake, with both glacier and lake dwarfed by the towering James Peak. It's a very peaceful, pretty and unique spot There are few places in the lower 48 states where you can get so close to a glacier without strenuous hiking or climbing. The walk to St. Mary's is not difficult; the round trip should take you about 1 1/4 hours, including the time spent at the glacier.

There are two ways to get to Central City from Idaho Springs. One is to take I-70 to Exit 240, then head north to Central City via Russell Gulch. This is the shorter way – the problem is that most of the route is unpaved and difficult to negotiate. If that sort of obstacle doesn't deter you, then go for it. Otherwise, take I-70 to Exit 244 and head up CO 119 to the town of Black Hawk. Take CO 279 for the final mile into Central City. The latter method is only 15 miles and won't take much longer than the shortcut. **Central City** developed almost overnight in 1859 with the discovery of gold in a narrow gulch and it became one of the wildest and richest of the mining communities. Two important relics of that era are **The Opera House** and the **Teller House**. The former is a lavishly decorated structure completed in the late 1870s and it looks as it did when people came from as far away as Denver to see performances by noted stars of the day. The tradition is still maintained with a summer-long opera festival. Tours of the Opera House last about 30 minutes. The equally lavish and large Teller House was built a few years prior to the Opera House to serve as a home for miners. It cost (for that day) an exorbitant figure – over $100,000. The community's wealth was flaunted, the front walk of the house was paved with gold bricks at one time to properly acknowledge the visit of the President of the United States! Today the interior of the Teller House has been converted to a casino (admission restricted to those over 21; minimum bet is $5). The current population of Central City is 300 people, a far cry from the good ol' days.

Return to Denver by reversing your route to I-70 and then heading east. Travel time back to the city is a little more than an hour.

A LOOP EXCURSION FROM COLORADO SPRINGS: This is another full-day, 120-mile loop that will bring you through some wonderful scenery and lead to a wide variety of other attraction The road should not present much of a problem for most dri although 20 miles are unpaved. The majority of it can be av by some backtracking that will add another 20 miles to th distance of this side trip. You'll begin by leaving Colorad via the familiar Midland Expressway (US 24). About 10

DENVER SUBURBS BEYOND GOLDEN: We mentioned earlie
that most of the attractions in Denver's suburbs were in Golden,
but beyond Golden there is a lot more to see, primarily in and
around the communities of **Idaho Springs** and **Central City**. This
is another one-day excursion that covers only 120 miles and offers
natural beauty as well as a closer look at Colorado's mining history.

Head west from Denver on I-70 to Exit 252 (about 25 miles from
downtown) at the town of El Rancho. Take CO 74 for three miles
and pick up the beginning of scenic CO 103. This road covers a
distance of 34 miles before ending in Idaho Springs. It traverses a
particularly scenic section of the **Pike National Forest**, including
the Squaw Pass and narrow Chicago Creek Canyon. Much of the
area is part of the Denver Mountain Parks System, so there are
frequent trails and roadside picnic areas. Including time for a few
stops and taking into account the slow speeds required on this
road, it should take you a little more than an hour to reach Idaho
Springs.

When the road reaches the Interstate you'll be right on the edge of
town and at the site of the **Argo Gold Mill**. This highly interesting
attraction lets you visit a gold mine from the late 1800s. It has long
since ceased operations but you'll come away with a much better
idea of how gold was mined during the boom times. You begin the
tour by picking up a hard hat and entering a hand-dug gold mine;
next, the mill and machinery that was used to process the ore is
explained. There is also a museum. At the conclusion of your visit,
which should take about 45 minutes, you are allowed to pan for
gold and other valuable stones in the creek, but it's likely that
you'll come away with anything of value other than the fun you
had.

If you haven't yet had enough of mines, you can visit the campus
of the **Colorado School of Mines** (Colorado Avenue and 8th
Street) and take a tour of the **Edgar Mine**. This mine is actually a
"classroom" that is used by the school to help students learn,
understand and actually devise mining techniques.

Idaho Springs' final attraction is a little difficult to get to. Take I-70
to Exit 238 (Fall River Road) and head 12 miles to the ghost town
of **Alice**. From this point you have to walk about three-quarters of
a mile to your destination – **Saint Mary's Glacier**. Here you will be
ble to view a glacier close up, probably glistening in the sun

is **Santa's Workshop-North Pole**, a fun-filled theme park with plenty of rides for the kids. The park is dominated by a huge ferris wheel, but a whimsical Santa's house is probably the highlight for most. You can easily spend two hours here but, unless you have children, it can be skipped.

Continue on US 24 for 22 miles until the town of Florissant where you will turn onto County Route 1 and the entrance to **Florissant Fossil Beds National Monument**. Well over 30 million years ago this 6,000-acre area was a lake. Volcanic ash covered it and preserved the plant and animal life in a thin layer of shale. Fossils of various types as well as petrified tree stumps are displayed in the Visitor Center along with detailed explanations of the geological processes which occurred here. Good views of the former lake can be had from some of the trails. Allow about an hour for the National Monument. County Route 1 is the unpaved part of this trip. If it didn't seem like a problem getting this far, then you can continue on this road all the way to the town of Cripple Creek. However, if the prospect of another 15 miles on it doesn't inspire you, then reverse your route on US 24 for 12 miles to the junction of CO 67 and head south until you reach Cripple Creek.

Cripple Creek was one of the most successful mining towns in all of Colorado. To look at this village of 600 souls today it is hard to imagine that it had as many as 18,000 residents in the 1890s. Over $350 million in gold was extracted from the surrounding area. As in Central City, Cripple Creek offers legal gambling, with the same age and dollar requirements.

The Cripple Creek & Victor Narrow Gauge Railway, pulled by an old coal-burning steam locomotive, will take you on a short (four-mile) excursion through the mining country to the neighboring town of Victor. Former mines are visible along the entire 45-minute route. Within the town itself is the **Cripple Creek Museum**, which describes the rise and fall of this boom town. An especially interesting feature is the recreated Assay Office in which the gold finds of the miners were weighed and certified. Located on the northern edge of town is the **Mollie Kathleen Gold Mine** where 45-minute tours lead you through an old mine that reaches more than 1,000 feet into the side of a mountain.

Entertainment 1890s style is available at the **Classic Victorian Melodrama** in the Imperial Hotel, which has been restored to its Victorian appearance. There are two-hour matinees and an evening performance, but you might want to think twice about driving back to Colorado Springs in the dark. On the other hand, you might not have time to see the afternoon performance if you visited Santa's Workshop.

Leave Cripple Creek via CO 67 northbound. This 20-mile stretch back to US 24 is on the western slope of Pikes Peak and affords dramatic views. From the junction of US 24 head east and you'll be back in Colorado Springs in under 40 minutes.

GRANBY TO RIFLE CUTOFF: This alternative route is 60 miles shorter than the main itinerary between these two points. While there is beautiful scenery along this route, the attractions are not quite as spectacular nor as numerous as on the main route which included Georgetown, Vail, Leadville, Aspen and Glenwood Springs. Therefore, rather than eliminating that part of the suggested itinerary, this cutoff is good for those on a short vacation who won't have time to get to the southern part of the state. Use this loop beginning at Granby and return to Denver along the main route at Rifle by reversing the itinerary through Georgetown. Then you can jump back to Denver.

This routing begins after Rocky Mountain National Park, taking US 40 westbound at the town of Granby. The beautiful route parallels the Colorado River for the next 26 miles. From that point it's 53 miles to Steamboat Springs, all of it equally scenic. You will cross the Continental Divide twice, once at Muddy Pass and again at Rabbit Ears Pass (elevations 8,722 and 9,426 feet, respectively).

Steamboat Springs is in an area containing well over 150 natural mineral springs. The town has extensive facilities for visitors who wish to take mineral baths or just swim in a pool fed by natural hot spring waters. The town is also a major winter sports center. This is evident at the huge skiing complex accessible via the **Steamboat Springs Ski Area & Gondola**. It provides visitors with scenic panoramas of the Yampa River Valley and surrounding mountain peaks. The gondolas will take you from town (elevation of 6,700 feet) all the way up to Thunderhead Peak (over 9,000 feet). Allow about an hour for this excursion.

Perhaps the scenic highlight of Steamboat Springs is a visit to **Fish Creek Falls** on the edge of town. A short path will take you from the parking area to a bridge that offers a fantastic view of the falls dropping 280 feet through a narrow crevice in the rocky cliffs.

Other trails lead through the pleasant forested area. A minimum of 45 minutes should be allotted to exploring the Fish Creek Falls area.

Steamboat Springs has many motels and resorts, all of which are quite expensive. Most are independent, but there is a **Best Western, Holiday Inn** and a **Sheraton Hotel**. Arrangements can be made in town for trips into the backcountry.

Upon leaving Steamboat Springs, you'll continue west on the still scenic US 40 for a distance of 42 miles to the town of Craig. On CO 13 in town is the **Museum of Northwest Colorado**. It contains information on local history and displays Indian artifacts. However, in addition to the usual exhibits found in these regional museums, this one has a large section devoted to the American cowboy. All of your favorite (and not so favorite) gun slingers are represented in the collection. At least 30 minutes is required to tour the museum. You'll find that Craig has a number of inexpensive motels if Steamboat Springs was beyond your budget.

Take CO 13 south from Craig. It is 90 miles to the town of Rifle and the junction of I-70 where you can pick up the main itinerary. CO 13 passes mostly through areas of wilderness and you won't encounter many towns. The scenery is nice, although not as dramatic as it was along US 40.

MONTROSE TO SALIDA CUTOFF: This routing covers 180 miles between the towns of Montrose and Salida, which is almost 250 miles less than the main itinerary via Silverton/Durango, Mesa Verde and Pagosa Springs. Again, you'll be missing a lot if you do take this route, but it can save two or more days if your time is limited. The trip is almost entirely via US 50 which means you'll see some outstanding scenery along the way.

Your route will diverge from the main itinerary after you have completed the Black Canyon of the Gunnison National Monument. Instead of heading west back to Montrose (eight miles away), go east. In 15 miles you'll reach the beginning of the beautiful 40-mile-long **Curecanti National Recreation Area**. Stretching along the Gunnison River, the area consists of three large reservoirs (Blue Mesa, Morrow Point and Crystal) that provide both recreational opportunities and great sightseeing. The first stop should be at the Cimarron Visitor Center where you can get information on activities and view the display of historical railroad equipment. From here a cutoff leads less than two miles to the **Morrow Point Dam**. You can tour the 469-foot-high dam, which is different in architectural style than most of the other large western dams, and stroll along Crystal Lake. US 50 continues east through the recreation area, providing frequent breathtaking views. Stop again at the Lake Fork Information Center and admire Blue Mesa Lake. A popular activity is to take a narrated boat ride on **Morrow Point Lake**. The spectacular ride through a dramatic canyon takes 1 1/2 hours and requires advance booking. Call (303) 641-0402 for reservations. Total time that you should plan on spending in Curecanti (excluding the boat ride) is about 2 1/2 hours.

(Since Curecanti National Recreation Area is not too far from the main route you may want to consider visiting it as part of the suggested itinerary and then turning around to rejoin the main route at Montrose.)

At the east end of the recreation area is the town of Gunnison. From here take CO 135 for 11 miles to the town of Almont and bear right along the Taylor River for another nine miles until you reach Taylor Reservoir. The 20-mile route from Gunnison is one of great beauty as it traverses a narrow canyon. The sheer rock walls on either side of you reach heights of 1,000 feet or more. Once you get to Taylor Reservoir you'll find one of the largest lakes in Colorado in an exquisite setting at the foot of the high Sawatch Mountain Range. Make your way back in the opposite direction to US 50 and head east one more time. It is 61 miles to the junction of Pagosa Springs and link-up with the main route. The entire road is picturesque, especially at Monarch Pass where US 50 winds its way across the Continental Divide amid heavily forested mountain slopes.

OTHER SIDE TRIPS: The remaining two alternative routes are side trips that branch off and return to the main route. The first one will add about 60 miles to the main itinerary in a trip for the adventurous. It heads to **Grand Mesa** and **Lands End**, not far from Grand Junction in the far western section of the state, and is partly via an unpaved road (for about 15 miles). It is moderately difficult and should not be done if you still have any qualms about mountain driving, although by this time you'll almost be a pro. Before arriving in Grand Junction, exit from I-70 onto CO 65 (Exit 49). Take this road into the **Grand Mesa National Forest**. Grand Mesa is reputed to be the world's largest flat-topped mountain, extending for over 30 miles at an altitude generally exceeding 10,000 feet.

Beautiful meadows and lush forests dot the top and there are also numerous deep canyons and dozens of lakes. The sights on the mesa are beautiful, but no more so than the immense panorama of western Colorado that lies beneath you. **Lands End** is the portion of Grand Mesa road where the world seems to suddenly drop off. Some quick directions on how to navigate through here. CO 65 will take you to the mesa's top about a mile past the town of Skyway. The unpaved road begins here to your right. Follow it along the mesa, stopping for the view of Lands End, and continuing once it becomes pavement at the end of the National Forest lands. A few more miles will bring you to US 50. Head west to Grand Junction where you can settle into town or rejoin the main itinerary for some sightseeing at the **Colorado National Monument**. Allow about three hours for this detour, more if you intend to make use of the extensive trail system along Grand Mesa.

The last side trip is more ambitious and can be done in one of two ways. The basic route covers a total of 145 miles, but only adds about 90 to the suggested main itinerary (you cut off some mileage by returning a different way from whence you came and wind up further along the route). From the town of Del Norte stay on US 160 for 34 miles, just past the town of Alamosa, until you reach the **Alamosa National Wildlife Refuge** (two miles south of the highway). Among the marshes you will see a large variety of birds, including ducks and geese. Bald eagles also frequent the refuge but, unfortunately, mostly in winter. If you're lucky you might see some at other times of the year. There are several easy walking trails that provide access to the marshes and overlooks as well as an informative Visitor Center. Allow about 45 minutes to an hour.

Continue on US 160 for 13 miles to CO 150 which heads north for 16 miles to one of Colorado's most amazing and awe inspiring sights – **Great Sand Dunes National Monument**. First, a few words to explain how the dunes got here. This is quite an arid area with sparse vegetation. Winds are able to carry sand from the surrounding area to this spot, but the weight of the sand cannot be lifted above the imposing Sangre de Cristo Mountains that form a barrier. The sand is deposited and slowly builds into a dune. These dunes now extend for more than 10 miles and reach staggering heights, some as high as 700 feet. Although winds continue to shift the sand, it is apparent that the major patterns have not changed much in the last hundred years. Your visit to Great Sand Dunes will include a stop at the Visitor Center and a stroll along the half-mile **Montville Trail** which shows the effects of the dunes on vegetation when the sand is blown away. You may also wish to climb some of the smaller dunes; the larger ones require a degree of expertise and stamina. The colors of the sand change as the day progresses, the most impressive times are sunrise and sunset when the sand becomes almost copper against the dark mountain background. But whatever the time of day and lighting conditions, it is a great sight. To see Great Sand Dunes as described will require about 90 minutes, more if you walk a lot of trails. Another alternative in summer is to take the 2 1/2-hour tour offered by **Great Sand Dunes Oasis**, which includes four-wheel-drive excursions into the dunes.

From the monument, retrace your route back to Alamosa via CO 150 and US 160 where you have a choice of paths. You may rejoin the main itinerary by proceeding north on CO 17 to the junction of US 285 at the town of Mineral Hot Springs. Or, you can extend this side trip by taking CO 17 south for 28 miles to the small town of Antonito. This is one of the terminals of the **Cumbres & Toltec Scenic Railroad**, an all-day excursion along and through the rugged San Juan Mountains. The trip ends in the town of Chama, New Mexico. Old locomotives pull the passenger coaches through magnificent scenery, much of which is totally inaccessible by road. It crosses several passes at elevations of greater than 10,000 feet. The return trip is by van. The extra 56-mile round trip from Alamosa is well worth the adventure of riding the Cumbres & Toltec. You can make reservations for the railroad by writing them at PO Box 668, Antonito, CO 81120. You might feel it is too similar to the Durango & Silverton Narrow Gauge. Your time and budget constraints may prevent doing both. Once you return to Alamosa follow the preceding directions to link with the main itinerary. If you have taken the train it will definitely be necessary to find a night's lodging on the side route and the choice is Alamosa. At least four major chain hotels are represented in town.

Chapter 2

Utah: Color Country

Nowhere else in America (perhaps even the world) will you encounter the unusual scenery that awaits you in Utah. The forces of erosion have created amazing formations of every imaginable shape and size. The dazzling array of colors that accompanies these creations has led to a large portion of the southern half of the state being aptly dubbed "Color Country."

This journey will take us through more than a dozen major areas of spectacular natural beauty, including several of America's most fascinating National Parks. Alternative side trips will lead you to even more outstanding landscape and intriguing history. The gateway and state capital, Salt Lake City, is a modern and attractive metropolis made even more interesting as it is also the capital of the Mormon faith.

Along the Suggested Itinerary

If you are driving into Utah from one of the surrounding states it's probable that you'll pick up the route somewhere other than our designated starting point of Salt Lake City, since its location in the center of the state (traveling east to west) means that other stops on the itinerary will be reached first. Possible exceptions to this are those entering Utah via I-80 or from the north on I-15. Both of these interstates lead to the heart of the city. Many of you may be flying into Salt Lake City International Airport, five miles west of downtown. From there you can pick up I-80 which heads east to downtown. In the central corridor of the city the two Interstates run along the same stretch. Exit 310 is the primary access to the downtown area.

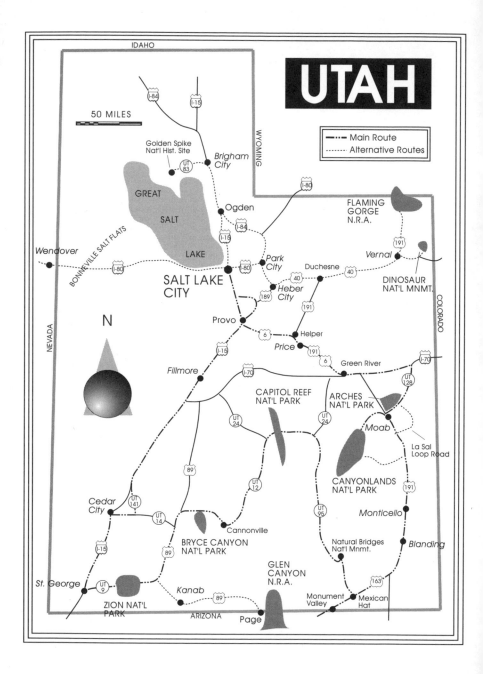

Salt Lake City is both the state capital and largest city, with a population of 160,000. At an altitude of 4,390 feet it is one of America's largest mountain cities. It is in a fine natural setting, adjacent to the lake and desert of the same name, with the beautiful Wasatch Mountains providing a dramatic backdrop.

As the headquarters of the Mormon church, a large number of its tourist attractions are related to the history and administration of that faith. That shouldn't deter non-Mormons one bit, for theirs is a compelling history and there is much to admire in the buildings erected to honor their beliefs.

Touring Salt Lake City is easy. A good many attractions are concentrated in the relatively small downtown area so you can soak up the atmosphere as you discover the sights. But whether you choose a car or your feet for transportation, the street system is easy to master. Temple Street North and Temple Street South run east and west and divide the numbered streets. Those north of Temple are 100 North, 200 North, and so forth. Those south of Temple are numbered the same, but with the South suffix. Main and State Streets run north to south so that streets west of Main are 100 West, 200 West, and so on, while those east of State are given an East designation. Get the picture? It makes getting lost practically impossible. There are some named streets that don't follow this simple pattern but most of them are not in the downtown area. With that geography lesson complete, let's begin our tour.

A sensible place to begin touring is at the **Salt Lake City Council Hall** (200 North and State Street). The Utah Travel Council is located here and the staff here will be happy to provide brochures and answer questions about seeing not only Salt Lake City, but all of Utah. Take a few moments to view the 1860s furniture and historical exhibits, as this building once served as City Hall.

To the north of Council Hall is the **State Capitol**. Perched on a hill overlooking the city, the Capitol is a good vantage point for looking out onto the city. The Capitol, dating from 1916, was built in the highly decorative Corinthian style. The design of the building is patterned after the national capitol. Marble and granite from Utah and other states were used in the fabulous construction. The rotunda contains murals relating to the state's history and attractive grounds complete the picture. You can take a guided tour when the legislature isn't in session. This allows you to see the legislative chambers, governor's reception room and other points

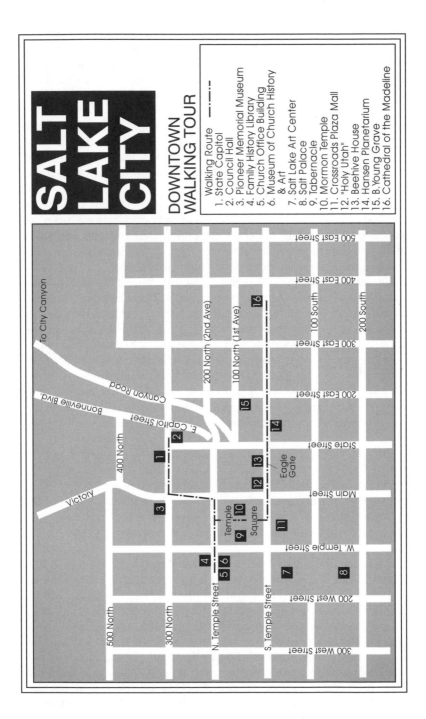

SALT LAKE CITY

DOWNTOWN WALKING TOUR

Walking Route —··—··—
1. State Capitol
2. Council Hall
3. Pioneer Memorial Museum
4. Family History Library
5. Church Office Building
6. Museum of Church History & Art
7. Salt Lake Art Center
8. Salt Palace
9. Tabernacle
10. Mormon Temple
11. Crossroads Plaza Mall
12. "Holy Utah"
13. Beehive House
14. Hansen Planetarium
15. B.Young Grave
16. Cathedral of the Madeline

of interest, though you can't wander about on your own. Allow about 45 minutes.

From the Capitol head down State Street to North Temple. Two blocks left at 50 N. Temple is the world headquarters of the Church of Jesus Christ of Latter Day Saints (LDS) – the official name of the Mormon church. The **Church Office Building** is a modern and sleek white tower with murals in the lobby depicting scenes from religious history. Guided tours will explain quite a bit about the church's organization and the functions that take place here. The tours finish on the 26th floor observation deck where you'll get a commanding view of the city and nearby mountains. On most days you'll also be able to see Great Salt Lake and the desert that lies to the city's west. With allowance for some time on the observation deck, you should plan on spending about an hour at the Church Office Building.

Head around the corner to the **Family History Library** at 35 N. West Temple. This is one of the world's greatest centers for genealogical research, with comprehensive records dating back to the middle of the 16th century. People of all faiths from around the world come here to trace their roots (an activity that is important in the Mormon faith). Assistance is available if you want to do some digging into your own family tree. The **Museum of Church History and Art** is next door at 45 N. West Temple. This interesting collection is by far the most all-encompassing chronicle of the development of the Mormon faith, covering every aspect of its history since Utah became the home of Mormonism. Allow approximately 45 minutes to see the museum.

Across the street from the museum is world famous **Temple Square**. It is the Mormon equivalent of the Vatican, Jerusalem and the Holy land combined into one. In keeping with its status as a place held sacred, you should conduct yourself in an appropriate manner here, regardless of your own beliefs. The square covers a whole city block, bounded by Main, North, South and West Temple Streets. Within the square are the Mormon Temple, Tabernacle, Assembly Hall, two Visitor Centers and numerous monuments that commemorate important events in Mormon history. The **Salt Lake Temple**, although closed to non-Mormons, is the most impressive of the structures within this walled enclave. Built of native granite from nearby Salt Lake City, it took almost 40 years to complete. The structure has six graceful spires, the highest of which soars a majestic 210 feet into the sky. A gold leaf statue of the Angel Moroni, measuring more than 12 feet high, stands atop the Temple. You can get an idea of what is inside by looking at some of the exhibits in the South Visitors Center. Informative tours of Temple Square leave frequently from here.

In the Visitor Center on the north side of the square are murals depicting scenes from the Old Testament. The upper level contains a large room that represents the universe. Standing in the center, at the end of a spiral ramp, is an 11-foot statue called Cristus. Entering the adjacent **Tabernacle**, which was built to hold many thousands of Brigham Young's followers, you'll see an unusual structure. The beams and connections are all wooden, though they rest on stone. The place can accommodate 6,500 people and is admired for its excellent acoustics. A highlight of every guided tour is the demonstration of literally hearing a pin drop even at the very back! The massive pipe organ is also justly famous. The Tabernacle is, of course, home of the Mormon Tabernacle Choir. The 300-plus singers can be seen during rehearsal. Check at the Visitor Center for schedules.

The most important monument in the Square is the **Sea Gull Monument**. This commemorates events in 1848 when the crops of Mormon settlers were threatened by hordes of crickets. The arrival of sea gulls from the west put an end to the threat. It was treated by Mormons as a miraculous event. Whether or not you're a believer, you'd better believe that a thorough visit to the many attractions of Temple Square will last 90 minutes or more.

To the immediate east of Temple Square is the "**Hotel Utah**." The quotes are necessary because it is no longer a hotel, having been converted to an office building to house part of the ever-growing LDS administrative apparatus. It was a world-class hotel for over 70 years and you can gather a sense of what it was like if you explore the very ornate Italian Renaissance lobby.

A block away is the **Beehive House** (67 E. South Temple). This was the home of Brigham Young and contains many original furnishings. Guided tours here last 30 minutes. Walking on nearby South Temple will bring you to a number of interesting sites. Spanning State Street is the **Eagle Gate**. It is a replica of the original and is topped by a huge eagle that has a 20-foot wingspan and weighs two tons. You might wonder why there is a gate here – the answer is that the original gate marked the entrance to property owned by Brigham Young. There is also a large statue of Brigham Young at

Main and South Temple but it's set in the middle of a busy intersection so you'll have to settle for a view from the curb. By the way,
you might have noticed by now that almost all of Salt Lake City's
streets are quite wide. This is because Brigham Young was a good
urban planner – he wanted all of the streets to be wide enough for
wagons to turn around. We need some of that kind of foresight
today.

Two blocks east at 331 E. South Temple is the **Cathedral of the
Madeline**, the largest non-Mormon house of worship in the state.
It has two towers more than 200 feet tall and the interior is filled
with Venetian mosaics, many different types of marble and statu-
ary carved from solid oak.

Our final downtown attraction is the **Hansen Planetarium** at 15 S.
State Street. In its Star Chamber you can experience a simulated
trip to the planets of our solar system. Those with less time may
want to limit themselves to the museum and exhibit hall where
there is much to learn about astronomy and space. Allow 30 minutes, or twice that much if you are going into the Star Chamber.

If you were walking to accomplish your downtown sightseeing
objectives, now is the time to get back into your car, as the next
three attractions are all located a distance east of the city center. The
University of Utah has a 1,200-acre campus in the foothills of the
Wasatch Mountains. It is the largest public institution of higher
education in the state and overlooks the city from its hillside perch.
The campus is attractive, most of it covered by an arboretum with
more than 7,000 trees. The campus boasts attractive gardens, a
natural history museum and the **Utah Fine Arts Museum**. You
may find that the European Renaissance and later works of art
somehow seem out of place in this setting. Nonetheless, it is a fine
museum. Time allocation depends on how many points of interest
within the University you plan to see, but figure at least an hour.
Behind the University is Fort Douglas, an active army installation.
The **Fort Douglas Military Museum** chronicles the history of the
army in the state as well as Utah's role in the U.S. Army.

When you leave the University or Fort Douglas, you'll reach Foot-
hill Drive. Take that for a mile to Sunnyside Avenue and turn left.
This heads out to **Emigration Canyon and Pioneer Trail State
Park**. This is the spot where Brigham Young first saw the Salt Lake
Valley. Despite initial disbelief from some of his followers,
Brigham Young is rumoured to have said "This is the right place,"

which evolved into the better known "This must be the place." Anyhow, it is the site of the colossal "This is the Place Monument," a 12-foot-high statue of Brigham Young and two other important church founders standing on a huge pedestal. Sculptures and plaques around the base fill you in on the history. The Monument also honors Spanish explorers who preceded the Mormons, traders, immigrants from California and others. Also within the park are a Visitor Center which details the Mormon migration to Utah, and a recreated pioneer village (authentic structures moved from various locations). The park can be seen in about 45 minutes, but allow more if you plan to stay around for craft demonstrations in the village of Old Deseret. Incidentally, Deseret was the name Mormons originally gave to the area we now know as Utah.

SALT LAKE CITY ODDS AND ENDS: The capital city is also the cultural and sports center of the state. A complex of buildings includes the **Salt Lake Arts Center**, the **Salt Palace**, and the ultra-modern **Symphony Hall**. All three are located diagonally across from Temple Square. Inquiries can be made at the box office or at Council Hall concerning events. You might want to take a walk around the complex just to admire the architecturally striking group of buildings.

Utah isn't known as a shopper's Mecca unless you're in the market for Indian-made hand-crafted jewelry. This and other local crafts are best bought in the southern portion of the state nearer to the Indian reservation. Regular shopping, if that's your thing on vacation, should be done here in the city. Two downtown locations are **Crossroads Plaza**, a 100-store-plus shopping mall on four levels directly across from Temple Square on South Main. It's very modern and quite attractive. The **ZCMI Mall** was one of America's first department stores, known as the Zion Cooperative Mercantile Institution, and used to be run by the Mormon church. The interior has now been completely renovated and converted into a mall with almost a hundred specialty shops, but the interesting original exterior facade remains.

One of the most unusual shopping areas is **Trolley Square**, which qualifies as an attraction in itself. As suggested by the name, this mall once served as the trolley barn for Salt Lake City's municipal trolley system. Saved from the wrecker, the 1908 structure now includes more than a hundred stores in addition to some vintage trolleys. Take note of the stained glass dome.

Recreational opportunities abound in and around the city on a year-round basis – the advantage of an urban area set so close to the mountains. **Liberty Park** is near downtown on 900 South and offers a wide variety of things to do. An amusement area and an interesting aviary are also on the grounds.

Among the many close-by ski areas are Alta, Brighton, Park City and Snowbird. They provide summer sightseeing opportunities as well but we'll describe those under excursions from Salt Lake City later in this chapter.

You may decide to spend at least a night in the vicinity, but choosing accommodations here is no problem. There is a wide variety to select from, in downtown, on the fringes or in nearby communities. Besides the usual chain establishments and a host of independent places, the most noted downtown lodgings are **Doubletree Hotel, Inn at Temple Square, Marriott Hotel**, and **Little America Hotel and Towers**. With the closing of Hotel Utah, Little America has taken over the distinction of being the city's most famous hotel (and also the largest). Quality restaurants can be found all over. The city has a much more cosmopolitan menu to choose from than you might expect. A good place to find an interesting selection of restaurants is in Trolley Square. Both hotels and restaurants are generally less expensive in Salt Lake City than in cities of comparable size throughout the U.S.

As beautiful as Salt Lake City is, you don't begin to truly experience Utah until you get away from the urban landscape. So now is a good time to get started on that part of our journey. Head south on Interstate 15 until you get to Exit 261 at the town of Spanish Fork, about 50 miles from downtown. On the way you'll pass Provo, a city with a number of attractions, but we'll describe the sights on the return trip to Salt Lake. Refer to that section now if you prefer.

At the I-15 exit take US 89 south for 14 miles to the town of Thistle. Turn left (eastbound) onto Highway 6. This is a good road that travels through several types of terrain, including mountains. In fact, the road takes you through Soldier Summit at an altitude of nearly 7,500 feet. Some 46 miles after joining US 6 you'll arrive at the small town of Helper. This unusual name for a town is derived from the small locomotives called "Helpers" that were based here to help trains make the steep ascent up to Soldier Summit. The railroad origins of Helper can still be seen today at the **Western**

Mining and Railroad Museum in the heart of town on Main Street. The building contains models of railroads and coal mines as well as displays of mining equipment. Two exhibits of special interest document the exploits of Butch Cassidy, who operated in this vicinity, as well as several tragic mine disasters that occurred in Utah. Allow about 45 minutes for your visit.

In downtown Main Street crosses Canyon Street. Head seven miles west on Canyon to Spring Canyon, an area of both scenic and historic interest. At the far end of the road are several ghost towns left from mining days. They are quite a sight – but just that; don't attempt to enter or touch because many of the buildings are unsafe. The round trip from town to the end of Spring Canyon with a visit to a couple of ghost towns can be done in about an hour to 90 minutes.

Continue east on US 6 (which is joined by US 191 just before Helper) for another eight miles until you reach the town of Price, seat of Carbon County. With a population of almost 9,000, Price is the biggest town in this part of the state. The two worthwhile attractions in town are both on Main Street (where else?). The first is the **Price Prehistoric Museum**. There are lifesize displays of dinosaurs, bones of a mammoth and a selection of colorful gems found in the area. The human history of Carbon County isn't ignored. You'll find displays of Indian artifacts from both long departed tribes like the Anasazi and modern ones, such as the Navajo and Ute. Among the most interesting exhibits are those of prehistoric Indian rock art. In the **Price Municipal Building** is a 200-foot mural depicting local history which is a brief but very interesting stop.

Consider staying overnight in Price, since you enter a large wilderness area upon leaving town which may make your visit too long for one day. About 10 decent motels dot the main strip in Price, among them a **Days Inn**.

From Price continue on US 6 East/US 191 South. It is 60 miles until you reach Interstate 70 just west of the town of Green River. The route to the Interstate travels on a large plateau with a view of the rugged Patmos Mountains and a number of canyons are encountered along the way. For almost two-thirds of the distance the road runs parallel to an ancient lava flow which you will catch glimpses of from time to time. Fill your tank before leaving Price as there are few signs of civilization along this road.

Take I-70 east for two miles to Exit 158 and follow the I-70 Business Route for two more miles into Green River.

In town on Main Street is the **John Wesley Powell Museum of River History**. This highly informative facility documents Powell's two exploratory trips on the Green and Colorado Rivers around 1870. As your travels in this part of the country continue, the name of John Wesley Powell will keep hitting you. His contributions to the exploration of the southwest were a major factor in later development of this area. The museum contains a few good examples of 19th century river boats, but the highlight is a multi-media show on the Green and Colorado Rivers. Since the two rivers have had a significant impact on the geology of all three states in this volume, this very fine presentation will provide you with a better understanding of the forces that have shaped the landscape. Allow about one hour for the museum, which includes the multi-media presentation.

The town of Green River lies at the southern end of the Gray Canyon and is set on the river's edge. This picturesque canyon has sheer cliffs and many unusual rock formations. Unfortunately, the drive of almost nine miles through the canyon is unpaved. However, as long as there hasn't been any recent rain and your car has good clearance, the road isn't overly difficult and you might want to venture at least a couple of miles along it to see this untouched wilderness.

There are also several notable sights of natural beauty within 20 miles of Green River on or adjacent to I-70 west of town. If you don't mind the extra mileage back and forth, you can take a trip to the **San Rafael Swell**, a 2,100-foot-high reef-like rock formation that extends for some 80 miles.

Finally, if you have the time, the town is an excellent starting point for a number of trips on the Green River. The methods of travel range from raft to motorized vessels, but any type will be sure to give you good close-up views of the canyon cut by the river. Some trips go as far as the river's junction with the Colorado, but that is a three-day affair! A number of operators offer one-day trips. The information center in town will provide details on the available trips, as well as places where you can rent your own boat for some individual exploration.

Backtrack two miles from Green River to rejoin Interstate 70 and head west on the highway, leaving it 44 miles later at Exit 202. Pick up **Utah 128**, a road that will carry you for 50 miles to Moab. The last 30 miles of this section, along a colorful sandstone gorge that has been carved by the Colorado River, will provide a fine introduction to the landscapes of southern Utah.

Milepost markers are measured from the junction with US 191, only two miles north of Moab's town center. There are several roadside picnic areas where you can take a relaxing break and enjoy the scenery.

At Milepost 21 there is a cutoff to the **Fisher Towers,** one of the area's most prominent landmarks. This unpaved road leads for just two miles to a picnic area. From this vantage point there is an excellent view of the three sandstone formations, the highest of which soars 900 feet above the valley floor. There is also a trail that leads around all three towers. Although the towers can be climbed, even the most experienced will find them challenging.

Continuing towards Moab you will come across another cutoff just beyond Milepost 16. This is the end of the La Sal Mountain Loop Road which is described in more detail in the Alternative Routes at the end of this chapter.

The river is not particularly wide along Utah 128, and in summer it will almost always have a muddy appearance. But don't underestimate its power – it is responsible for the beauty of the gorge you are traveling through and for many other even more spectacular sights as you continue on your journey.

At the junction of US 191 turn left and in a couple of minutes you'll be in Moab. Moab is the largest town in this part of the state. It makes sense for you to seek overnight accommodations here as the choice is much greater than anywhere else in this region. More important, Moab is in the heart of the canyon country and it makes an excellent base for exploring the National Parks and other attractions of the area.

Major chains such as **Best Western, Ramada** and **Super 8** are represented here, and there are more than a dozen non-affiliated motels to choose from. Restaurants range from the fast-food variety to the elegant, with a cowboy-style chuck wagon supper and after-dinner show somewhere in the middle. Moab is also the headquarters for various tours of the area by boat, four-wheel-drive vehicle and other methods.

There are several rafting and canoe trips lasting from a half-day to several days. The off-road and 4WD tours are a good idea if you want to really see the backcountry but don't want to ruin your car. Most car rental agencies specifically prohibit use of their rental cars from any use off regular roads. The backcountry excursions are also good for those who aren't quite daring enough to try it on their own. The rewards are great and you'll enjoy an outing with any of the tour operators. Information can be obtained from the Moab Visitor Center at 805 N. Main Street.

One boat tour that is different from the others is **Canyonlands By Night**. This 90-minute trip leaves every night at sunset from just off US 191 at the bridge over the Colorado River. Geological and local history are pointed out as the boat makes its way several miles up the river. Darkness has fallen by the time you begin the return trip downstream and there is a moving sound and light show on the canyon walls (and moving is meant to be taken literally!).

There are a couple of worthwhile attractions in or close to Moab. The first, in town, is the **Dan O'Laurie Museum**. There is no admission to see the interesting exhibits on Moab's past, both recent and ancient.

Located 15 miles south of town on US 191 is the unique **Hole In The Rock**. An enterprising individual built (it would be more accurate to say excavated) his 14-room home in the side of a sandstone cliff. You may think this sounds like some corny Fred Flintstone exhibit for kids, but it's a real house that real people lived in and it makes for a fascinating visit.

We mentioned that Moab is the logical starting point for touring the canyon country – Arches National Park, Canyonlands National Park and a number of smaller state parks and reserves. The order you do them in doesn't matter, but keep in mind that it's much more comfortable to do the bulk of your outdoor activity in the morning whenever possible to avoid the blazing summer after-noons.

Both **Arches National Park** and **Canyonlands National Park** are reached by a short drive north of Moab. You should allow a

half-day to see Canyonlands and at least that much for Arches –
more if you are going to be doing some of the longer trails. It's a
wise idea to carry drinking water for any summertime walks that
will last more than a half-hour. As a matter of fact, it comes in
handy even when taking short strolls.

We'll start with **Canyonlands**. Take US 191 for 10 miles to UT 313.
You'll reach Canyonlands after 20 miles of travel on a good road
that rises through the canyon country and offers excellent views
along the way.

The park encompasses a large area surrounding the confluence of
the Green and Colorado Rivers. These waterways effectively cut
the park into three distinct sections named Islands in the Sky, The
Needles, and The Maze, none of which are interconnected by road.
We'll concentrate on Islands in the Sky, the most accessible of the
three and the only one with a good road system. The Maze is
wilderness backcountry where even four-wheel-drive vehicles
provide only limited access. The Needles can be reached without
difficulty, but it's a long drive from the Islands section. For those
of you who are interested, information on visiting The Needles will
be found in the Alternative Routes portion of this chapter.

Soon after entering Canyonlands National Park you'll reach the
Visitor Center, which has interesting exhibits and trail information.
After touring the Visitor Center you'll soon arrive at the **Shafer
Canyon Overlook**. From here you see not only an exceptional
landscape, but the old mining roads that twisted their way through
the deep narrow canyons below. There is a trailhead here, but it's
a long and difficult trip, as are most of Canyonland's trails. Many
of them involve drops (and, therefore, even more strenuous return
climbs) of 2,000 feet or more. Some exceptions are noted below and
there are several short trails along the road leading to the canyon
rim.

Soon after the overlook the road splits to the north and south. The
road south only lasts a few miles but there is plenty to see. At the
White Rim Overlook there is a trail by the same name; it's a bit
over a mile long and relatively easy. The main attraction in this
direction comes at the end of the road when you reach **Grand View
Point**. One of the most outstanding views in all of Utah awaits you.
On a clear day (the rule rather than the exception in this part of the
country) you will see a large part of Canyonlands National Park,
including portions of The Needles and Maze sections serving as the

foreground for distant mountains. Below is the snake-like path of the Colorado River. The colorful canyon walls are a natural museum, revealing thousands of years of history, each neatly arranged in its own clearly visible layer. **Grand View Trail** is under two miles long and leads to more unforgettable views.

Proceeding now in the opposite direction it's 10 miles to the road's northern terminus. The main attraction here is the **Upheaval Dome**, reached by the easy **Crater View Trail**. Upheaval Dome extends several miles across, a gigantic rock pile that must have been created by a source of unimaginable power. It is now thought to be the result of a meteor impact.

Near Canyonlands, and a most worthwhile stop either on the way to or from the Park, is **Dead Horse Point State Park**. This small area (compared to Canyonlands) is a miniature Islands in the Sky. Standing almost half a mile above the Colorado River you have further evidence of the various eras in the geologic history of the earth. The name of the park has several different origins, but most historians agree it has something to do with horses that were trapped in the canyon and died from a lack of water, despite the proximity of the unreachable river.

Arches National Park is even closer to Moab than the Canyonlands, the entrance being only six miles north of the town center, also on US 191. Within the harsh but colorful landscape are nearly 90 natural arch formations, said to be the largest concentration of arches in the world. Your first stop should be the Visitor Center, which is reached minutes after entering the park. The majority of the arches and other unusual formations are visible from the park's excellent road system. Including doubling back (the main road and all spurs that lead from it are deadends), you'll cover close to 60 miles within the park's borders.

Many of the interesting geological oddities are adjacent to the road or accessible by a short walk. These include the Tower of Babel, the Rock Pinnacles and Balanced Rock. You won't appreciate how appropriate their names are until you see them! Panorama Point, Salt Valley and Fiery Furnace Overlook all provide splendid views of the colorful desert and towering mountains. The two arches most easily seen from the roadside are those at Delicate Arch Viewpoint and Skyline Arch.

Arches National Park affords ample opportunity for walking and hiking. Trails too numerous to mention dot the park. Most are several miles in length or more and many are made more difficult by steep grades and sandy terrain. Both the Windows Trail and the trail to Landscape Arch (the park's largest and arguably the most beautiful) are especially worth the trip and are not overly difficult.

There is one flat, easy trail that is a must. This is the **Park Avenue Trail**, the reference being to New York's Park Avenue. Here the skyscrapers are replaced by sheer rock formations in a variety of hues lining both sides of the broad trail. The Three Gossips formation is the most interesting of all along this one-mile walk (each way).

Putting the canyons and arches behind us, we depart Moab via US 191, heading south into the state's southeastern corner. But don't think you have completely left behind the scenery of Arches and Canyonlands, for this good road crosses colorful high desert with mountains visible in the distance on either side. **Wilson Arch** is one of many features you will encounter on this route. It's located about 22 miles south of Moab.

There are a number of unusual scenic attractions on roads branching off US 191. Most are difficult to reach because of poor roads, steep climbs, or both. Some of the more readily reached destinations are described under Alternative Routes.

US 191 itself is an excellent artery, well paved, with gentle grades and little traffic to interfere with the view or ease of driving. All of the towns it passes through are small but food and lodging can be found in, among others, Monticello, Blanding, Mexican Hat and Gouldings. The town of Blanding is 75 miles south of Moab and its main attraction, **Edge of the Cedars State Park**, is right off the highway at the north edge of town. Contained within the park are the ruins of an Anasazi Indian community dating from 1000 A.D. The ruins, which are being restored, can be seen from an observation tower and a trail that passes by the remains of dwellings and ceremonial sites. There is also a museum that displays Anasazi artifacts and those of more recent Indian cultures. Allow about an hour for this attraction, less if you won't be hitting the trail.

Continue on US 191 to the junction of US 163 right after the town of Bluff. Follow US 163 until you reach **Mexican Hat**, a distance of almost 50 miles from Blanding. This town gets its name from a large rock formation that does resemble a sombrero turned upside down.

The most interesting attraction in this area is the **Goosenecks State Park**, four miles north and then three miles west via UT 316. This small park with very limited facilities will surprise you – you won't be expecting anything as the road ends at a tiny parking area with apparently nothing to be seen. By walking a few steps to the edge of the rim and looking down – behold! The San Juan River, a thousand feet below and filled with silt, snakes over a distance of six miles in a series of sharp curves that, from point to point only cover a mile.

Heading 25 miles south on US 163 delivers you to the doorstep of Gouldings, little more than a trading post with tourist facilities added on. Its importance now is as the gateway to one of America's most recognizable scenes – the **Monument Valley Navajo Tribal Park**. Many TV ads, dozens of car commercials among them, are filmed here. You will understand why when you travel through this beautiful valley. The park belongs to the Navajo Indians and is almost entirely in Arizona, but we include it here not only because you enter it through Utah, but because it logically goes with the touring route we've been following.

Monument Valley (where even the valley lies at an elevation over 5,000 feet) is a wonderful example of the forces of erosion acting upon the soft sandstone rock. Time has left huge pinnacles and buttes standing like giant sentries near the sandy surface. Like many other places, the color of the rocks seems to change as the day goes by, but it's best known for its deep reddish-brown hues.

The best way to see the valley is via the 17-mile **Monument Valley Drive**. It allows you to get close-up views of the most noted formations. Despite the dirt surface (which can become difficult to get through if it has just rained) it's readily passable most of the time without special vehicles. Alternatively, guided tours of the valley are available, some of which go well beyond the territory covered by the scenic drive. The Navajo have built an interesting Visitor Center at the beginning of the drive. The balcony offers impressive views of the valley for those short of time. Allow close to two hours if you are going to be doing the drive on your own.

From Monument Valley it will be necessary to retrace your route back north on US 163 to just past Mexican Hat where UT 261 begins. Take the latter road north until the junction of UT 95 and make a left. Two miles further is the cutoff to **Natural Bridges National Monument**. The total distance from Gouldings is 66 miles.

At the Visitor Center there are exhibits on how the natural bridges were formed. You will also see a large solar power demonstration project (the power produced here runs the Visitor Center). Then it's time to embark on the nine-mile loop road that passes the three bridges of the monument. Before reaching the first bridge you'll also encounter the magnificent panorama of **Monument Valley Overlook**.

Owachoma is the oldest of the bridges and is just over 100 feet high and less than 200 feet across. Erosion has worn it down so that its thickness is only a few feet. Massive Kachina is the toddler of the trio; it exceeds 200 feet in both height and width. The largest bridge is Sipapu at 220 feet high and almost 270 feet across. Allow one hour for the drive and view stops. You can extend your visit by taking the trails from the bridge viewpoints down to the bridges themselves, but they are generally long, difficult treks. Owachoma is the easiest to reach if you want to give one a try.

Once you rejoin UT 95 (right turn at the end of UT 275), there is a 100-mile stretch of highway with almost no sign of civilization. Make sure your car has enough gas and be sure to carry drinking water with you. In summer it's also a good idea to carry some extra water for the car, because breaking down here is no fun. On the brighter side, the road is decent and you'll be traveling through the scenic Henry Mountains. There is an especially nice section at Cataract Canyon as the road passes through a remote part of Glen Canyon National Recreation Area.

Once you reach the town of Hanksville you'll find all the necessary services, including food and lodging. As UT 95 ends, go west (left) on UT 24 and you'll soon reach the next destination, Capitol Reef National Park. The total distance from Natural Bridges to the Visitor Center at Capitol Reef is 143 miles. You'll probably have spent the last night somewhere in the vicinity of Monument Valley. By the time you reach the park it might well be late in the day. If you're looking for a place to stay try Hanksville (east of the Park), Torrey and Bicknell (west), all along UT 24.

It is only during the past few years that **Capitol Reef National Park** has had any significant development of facilities. It still is largely a primitive area, but one that can be seen.

Capitol Reef was formed by an uplifting of the earth. The result is a remarkable ridge over 1,000 feet high that stretches for nearly 100 miles. It looks almost like a huge ocean reef, hence the second part of the name. The white-colored top of the reef reminded someone of the Capitol Dome in Washington. The rest of the reef has a remarkable variety of colors and the area is filled with canyons and rock formations of various types.

Begin your discovery at the Visitor Center along UT 24. A rough and unpaved road runs along the entire length of the rim, providing spectacular views and access to numerous trails. Some of you might want to attempt it, but for the majority of visitors there is a paved scenic road lasting seven miles (one-way) that is a miniature version of the longer road. Allow about 90 minutes for the shorter trip and stop at the Visitor Center, with additional time if you are going to explore some of the trails.

Eleven miles west of Capitol Reef is the town of Torrey. It marks the beginning of UT 12, one of the nation's most spectacular drives. The highlight of this drive is a 30-mile section known as the **Boulder-Escalante Scenic Drive**. This begins in the small town of Boulder, 30 miles south of Torrey.

Before beginning this portion of the drive you will come upon the **Anasazi State Park**. This is another fine archaeological site from around 1100 A.D. In addition to a museum with artifacts, you can walk through the excavated village and a replica of an Anasazi pueblo. The community once numbered several hundred inhabitants in about 50 buildings. As with many other such sites in Utah, Colorado and Arizona, it is not known why the villagers left, although food shortage is one of the probable causes. A thorough visit will take approximately 45 minutes.

The town of Boulder is very small, with less than a thousand residents, but gas and food are available. As you drive the Boulder-Escalante Highway there is a constantly changing panorama of canyons and mountains, enhanced by an endless variety of colors. Just past Escalante is another member of the excellent state park system, the **Escalante Petrified Forest State Park**. Allow one full hour to walk the mile-long loop known as the **Wide Hollow Trail**.

You'll see countless examples of petrified wood. Far less famous than the Petrified Forest of Arizona, this Park nevertheless does contain beautiful examples of wood that have turned to stone. Impurities in virtually every piece of rock add a sparkling dash of color, a visual oddity that makes them appear as gems rather than stone.

Once you leave the Park it is about 30 miles to the town of Cannonville, sometimes referred to as Gun Shot because it's too small to have a cannon. (Honest, we didn't make that up!) Leave UT 12 following signs for nine miles until you reach **Kodachrome Basin State Park**. As the name says, it's a place where the cliffs come in a fabulous array of colors. More fascinating still are the sand pipes, pillars of rock ranging in height from that of a human adult to as high as a 15-story building. Dozens of them are named to reflect some object that people thought they looked like. They contain hard minerals that were apparently left standing when the surrounding rock was eroded away over eons.

There are a number of short trails that require only a minor amount of climbing. These include the **Nature Trail**, **Angel's Place Trail**, **Grand Parade Trail** and the **Arch Trail**, the latter leading to a large natural arch. There are also longer and more difficult trails for those whose fascination with the land demands further exploration. In any event, a minimum of 90 minutes is necessary to do justice to the park.

Continue west on UT 12 (left) for 12 miles which will bring you to the settlement of Ruby's Inn (it's not big enough to call a town). A left turn here and one more mile brings us to the next National Park on our sojourn.

There is little doubt that Utah, as you've already discovered by now, has some of the world's most unusual and beautiful sights. It can be argued that **Bryce Canyon National Park** is the best of the best. While individual tastes vary, most are deeply impressed by what they see here.

This bowl-shaped natural amphitheater contains a mind boggling array of rock formations including tens of thousands of spires and pinnacles. Pink, red, rust and other colors enhance the beauty of the shapes and no place looks the same in the afternoon as it did in the morning! It will leave you feeling as if you are in an unreal world – a fairy tale setting that can be touched. It is the kind of place where you could stand in one spot and stare out for hours. Some say this special place reduces them to tears.

Before discussing the sites of Bryce here are a few words about the accommodations in the area. There are no large towns, but motels are located right outside the park (including a large **Best Western**) and in the nearby towns of Tropic, Hatch and Panguitch. You can also stay inside the park at the rustic **Bryce Canyon Lodge**, but reservations have to be made far in advance. Contact TW Services (see last section of the book). There are plenty of restaurants in the area and non-guests can dine at the Bryce Canyon Lodge.

What makes a visit to Bryce even more enjoyable is the fact that it's very easy to tour. A paved road runs for 20 miles from the entrance to the park's southern end. With side spurs the total driving in the park is about 50 miles. Short walks from roadside parking areas lead to overlooks in over a dozen places. The view from any of them is incomparable. Included in the "must see" category are Farview Point, Natural Bridge, Ponderosa Point, Yovimpo Point and Rainbow Point (all on the main road) and Fairyland View, Sunrise Point, Sunset Point, Inspiration Point, Bryce Point and Paria View (all on short spurs from the main road).

The park also offers plenty of opportunity for walking and hiking. The **Rim Trail** runs for over five miles along the rim, paralleling the road. The section between Sunrise and Sunset Points is especially popular. The **Under the Rim Trail** runs for 22 miles and comprises a number of other trails including the Navajo Loop, Fairyland and Tower Bridge Trails. These trails can involve descents below the rim of more than 700 feet, so be sure you're physically capable of making the strenuous return climb. Also keep in mind that Bryce's rim lies at an altitude of between 8,000 and 9,000 feet. An easier descent (only about 300 feet) is the 1 1/2-mile long **Queens Garden Trail** at Sunrise Point. Any walk below the rim (even if it's only a small portion of the trail) will give you a completely different perspective of the maze of rock formations than you get while standing at the top and peering down. One thing is certain – the view from either vantage is one that you'll never forget!

A visit to Bryce will take at least a half-day, even if you are just going to do the drive and walk to the overlooks or part of the Rim Trail. Plan on an entire day for visits that include going beneath the rim.

You won't want to leave Bryce, but when you do the scenery won't stop. Exit the park and continue west on UT 12. You enter the **Dixie National Forest** (which you also passed through during the Boulder-Escalante Drive) in a section known as **Red Canyon**. This 14-mile stretch of road connects Bryce with US 89 and is very appropriately named. The red sandstone rock that lies on both sides of the road makes for a most pleasant drive and there are a number of pullouts if you want to step out of the car and take it all in. One particularly beautiful area is set next to a series of tunnels, about half-way between Bryce and the junction of US 89. There are also several trails that depart from the pullouts but most are not for the inexperienced hiker. You can get further information from the Forest Supervisor.

At US 89 turn left (southbound), passing through the towns of Hatch, Long Valley Junction and Orderville before reaching Mt. Carmel Junction. US 89 is a good road providing views of distant mountains, but it doesn't compare to the sights found on UT 12. There are, however, plenty of services available along this stretch of the road, a distance of 42 miles.

Upon reaching Mt. Carmel Junction turn right on UT 9. The next 23 miles are known as the **Zion-Mt. Carmel Highway,** and it not only provides scenery that does compete with UT 12, but it's acknowledged as one of the nation's great road engineering achievements.

The first half of the ride on the Highway is outside of the domain of **Zion National Park**. On reaching the East Entrance of the park the scenery becomes even more spectacular and the ride gets more exciting. It's the last few miles that have made it famous, as the Zion-Mt. Carmel Highway drops down to reach the junction with Zion Canyon. But there are attractions along the road before reaching that point, so let's not jump the gun.

Checkerboard Mesa is one of the park's many famous features. This low and sloping formation features a crisscross pattern of fractures in the rock that does resemble a game board. There are two tunnels along this section of the road, the first measuring only 500 feet. Zion Tunnel, the second one, is over 10 times that length. At the east end of the tunnel the Canyon Overlook Trail begins, an easy one-mile walk that leads to a spectacular view of the canyon.

As you drive through Zion Tunnel you'll notice that there are "windows" cut through the rock. In days gone by when the park was far less crowded you were allowed to peer through these windows and view portions of the canyon, but stopping is no longer permitted and is, in fact, very dangerous. A series of six switchbacks begins as soon as you emerge from the tunnel. Go slow, not only because of the sharp turns and fairly steep descent (the road is in excellent shape and not a problem to drive), but because you'll want to admire the beauty that surrounds you. There is a parking area amid the switchbacks where you can catch your breath, savor the colorful mountains and marvel at the road above and beneath you.

The junction with the Zion Canyon Road will be reached when you get to the bottom. Zion National Park's interesting Visitor Center is located here. After stopping for a while at the center you'll be ready to tour Zion Canyon, the park's best known area.

The **Canyon Drive** is only a few miles long but the sights literally come one after the other. Among the formations that you'll see from the many roadside pullouts (or on short trails from the parking areas) are the Towers of the Virgin, the East Temple, Twin Brothers, Mountain of the Sun, Altar of Sacrifice, the Beehives, the Sentinel, the Court of the Patriarchs and the most famous of all of Zion's landmarks, the Great White Throne. It's obvious that the park's earliest visitors, Mormon settlers, were impressed with what must have surely seemed to them to be God's country. The road ends at the Temple of Sinawana, which is an amphitheater containing two large boulders called the Altar and the Pulpit.

Zion also has many trails. Two popular ones are **Weeping Rock** and **Gateway to the Narrows**, the latter beginning at the Temple of Sinawana. Both are easy trails along the Virgin River in a narrow canyon, lush with vegetation. The Narrows Trail begins where the Gateway ends, but this trail, although also fairly easy, is still 16 miles long. You can walk part of it if you're still ambitious after completing the Gateway, but be aware that thunderstorms can create flash floods here. These present a real danger in the extremely narrow canyon – sometimes as little as 20 feet wide. Leave immediately if the weather looks threatening.

Zion has one other section that is worth a visit. This is in the northwest corner of the Park and is called Kolob Canyon. However, it isn't connected to the rest of the park by road, so we'll defer description of it until later in our journey.

The time required to do the Canyon and Mt. Carmel Highway sections of Zion again depends on the extent of your hikes, but a minimum of a half-day is necessary to do it justice. A full day is better.

There are ample hotels and places to eat in the vicinity of Zion, concentrated in the town of Springdale, outside the park entrance to the south of the junction of the Canyon and Mt. Carmel roads. Within Zion itself is **Zion Lodge**. As was the case with Bryce Canyon Lodge, staying here requires reservations far in advance. This establishment is also run by TW Services. An even wider choice of places to be stay can be found in St. George, a distance of 40 miles from the Visitor Center, and our next destination.

Upon leaving Zion, turn right on UT 9 which will lead you west. The road will continue with scenic views of brownish red mountains, cliffs and ridges as it descends gently to the town of Hurricane. It ends 10 miles past that point at Interstate 15. Take I-15 south for eight miles to Exit 8 and the town of St. George (population 30,000). This is the unofficial capital of Utah's "Dixie" country, so-called because of its mild climate. (They even grow some cotton here.) Several **Best Westerns**, **Comfort Inns**, **Holiday Inns** and **Ramadas** are located here and there is even a **Hilton** for those seeking greater luxury. Besides the restaurants within major hotels, there are numerous other choices concentrated on St. George Blvd.

The **St. George Temple** of the LDS Church in the center of town (400 East and 200 South Streets) is a beautiful white structure completed in 1877 and is much admired architecturally. Like all Mormon temples it's closed to non-Mormons, but you can visit the attractive grounds. It's especially beautiful at night when soft lighting shines upon it. The nearby Tabernacle is open to the public. Explanatory tours leave from the Temple's Visitor Center, but if you've taken the more comprehensive tour in Salt Lake City it isn't necessary to repeat it here.

Among St. George's historic attractions are the **Daughters of Utah Pioneer Museum**, with a wealth of artifacts illustrating local history, and the **Brigham Young Winter Home**, furnished to the period. These are next to one another on St. George Blvd. Although Brigham Young did spend many of his winters in the mild climate here during his later years, a more important figure in local Mormon history is represented at the **Jacob Hamblin House**, four miles northwest of town via Sunset Blvd. Hamblin was instrumental in the early settlement of Mormon farmers in this part of the state.

The city of St. George is surrounded by mountains and a short drive north on UT 18 (nine miles) provides access to outstanding beauty in **Snow Canyon State Park**. This six-mile canyon, with walls towering more than 500 feet above the valley floor, encompasses a variety of terrains and geologic features. It is in a desert, complete with sand dunes, but there are also deep red sandstone mountains that form the canyon and lava flows from ancient volcanoes. Most of this can be seen from the park overlook on UT 18, but UT 300 goes into the canyon. At the bottom are trails of varying lengths, but beware of the heat during summer afternoons. Allow more than a half-hour if you are going to be walking in the canyon.

When leaving St. George head back north on I-15. The 30-odd miles to Exit 40 will take only a half-hour. From here is immediate access to the **Kolob Canyon** section of Zion National Park. There is a small Visitor Center and a five-mile scenic drive passing through the Finger Canyons (the name given to the dominant rock formation in this area) and ending at the Kolob Canyon Overlook, a panorama rivaling any of those seen in the much more heavily visited main section of Zion.

After returning to I-15, continue north for less than 20 miles to Exit 59 at Cedar City. This tidy community is quite a bit smaller than St. George but, because it is a major tourist center, there are lodging and dining facilities that equal those of its big sister to the south. Most of the chains in St. George are also represented here.

Besides being a gateway to the nearby scenic areas, **Cedar City** is known as the home of the **Utah Shakespearean Festival**, held from early June through September on the campus of Southern Utah University. Those in the know say that performances here are first class. If you're interested in attending a performance, schedules and tickets are available form the Box Office, Utah Shakespearean Festival, Cedar City UT 84720. Performances are held in a large theater reminiscent of those from Elizabethan England.

An added attraction is the free **Greenshow** held at 7:30 each night (except Sunday). Minstrels, jugglers, singers and dancers perform on the large university green, costumed in period. It's fun for

children and adults and doesn't require that you have an appreciation or understanding of Shakespeare.

Head east from Cedar City on UT 14 until you get to the junction
of UT 148. This 18-mile drive rises sharply in some places (most
notably as it leaves town), bringing you up to an elevation of over
9,000 feet. Shortly after crossing the 9,900-foot mark at Midway
Summit, turn left onto UT 148. Then it's only a few miles to Cedar
Breaks National Monument.

Cedar Breaks is a remarkable place, resembling Bryce Canyon in
many ways. (That's easier to understand when you realize that it's
part of the same geologic formation.) Besides being a lot smaller,
it's almost 2,000 feet higher than Bryce. While lacking the size and
diversity found in Bryce, its beauty requires no apology to any
competition. The amphitheater is three miles across and 2,500 feet
deep. Impurities in the rock strata produce a dazzling array of
colors. There is a five-mile scenic drive near the rim and several
overlooks, in addition to a Visitor Center. The majority of trails
parallel the rim, but there is one that drops below. Remember that
at this altitude any walking requires a slower pace to compensate
for the thinner air. Those not in good physical condition are better
off restricting themselves to the overlooks. About 45 minutes to an
hour will provide ample time to drive along the rim and absorb the
sights.

Continue north on UT 148 when departing Cedar Breaks. You'll
pass the town of Brian Head, one of Utah's most famous ski resorts
(summer accommodations available at lower prices). For the more
adventurous there is a drive to the top of **Brian Peak** from which
there is a view of southern Utah stretching for a hundred miles in
every direction. The road is passable only in good weather. About
20 miles north of Cedar Breaks is the town of Parowan, where
you'll again hook up with I-15 heading northbound.

There aren't any major attractions from this point until you reach
the Provo area, but the distance of 190 miles is all by fast Interstate
and can be covered in about three hours. The road parallels the
Mineral and Pahvant Mountain ranges in the southern portion and
the Wasatch Range as you head further north, so the scenery isn't
bad. There are plenty of rest stops and restaurants are plentiful
along the route. If your plans call for an overnight stop on this
stretch the best choice of accommodations will be found in the
communities of Beaver, Fillmore or Nephi.

Beaver is one of Utah's oldest towns with many historic buildings dating from the 1850s. You can get information on a walking tour at the information center on Main Street (Exit 112).

The town of Fillmore was the capital of the Utah Territory, chosen by Brigham Young in 1851 because of its central location. Exit 163 will bring you into town and the **Territorial State House State Park**. The building dates from 1855 and contains exhibits concerning its role in Utah history. The small structure is one wing of a much larger four-wing building. Also located here are log cabins and a small schoolhouse dating from the Territorial capital period.

Take Exit 266 off of I-15 into **Provo**. This is Utah's second largest city, with a population of approaching 85,000. An attractive community, it's primarily a college town. The setting is typical of Utah – mountains hemming it in on all sides, though the west side of the town faces Utah Lake, the largest body of fresh water in the state.

No fewer than six major lodging chains are represented, so finding a place to stay is no problem. There is also a wide range of independent hostelries to choose from. Getting around is easy as Provo has a simple numbered grid pattern with location indicated by the direction in the street name.

Among the attractions in town are the **Provo Temple**, newest of the major Mormon temples. Like many others it's a brilliant white color (also illuminated at night) and is set on attractive grounds. The temple is on N. Temple Drive in the extreme northeastern corner of the city, overlooking the rest of Provo from its hillside locale. The **McCurdy Doll Museum** (on N. 100 East Street) has a collection of more than 4,000 dolls representing famous women (including First Ladies and women of the Bible) and a folk doll collection of women of just almost every nationality you can think of. Allow approximately 30 minutes.

If you're looking for a change of pace from sightseeing and want some recreation, the **Saratoga Resort** is the place to go. It's in the adjacent town of Lehi (take I-15 to Exit 282, then UT 73 and local streets, following signs for four miles). On the north shore of Utah Lake, the amusement park features rides, mini golf, water slides and other activities. There are several large swimming pools with warm mineral water fed by natural springs. A minimum of two hours should be allocated to this attraction, probably a lot more if you are traveling with children, who will surely need a break from scenery that is more appreciated by adults.

Further recreational opportunities abound at **Utah Lake State Park**, located west of downtown at the very end of Center Street, which divides the North and South streets of Provo. The lake is about 24 miles long and nearly 11 wide, but it only averages ten feet deep. Besides boating, swimming and other water-related activities, migratory bird watching is popular in this lovely mountain-ringed setting.

Provo is known throughout the country as the home of **Brigham Young University**. One of the largest church-supported educational institutions in the world, it has high academic standards, a strict code of ethics, and even a dress code. The students don't look like those you would see at other American universities, except for military academies, but there aren't any uniforms here. BYU, as it's commonly known, or "The Y" as evidenced by the big white letter drawn on the nearby mountainside, is probably best known outside of Utah for the success of its football team and, to a lesser extent, basketball. Several NFL quarterbacks starred for the Cougars. The attractive campus covers more than 600 acres. You can explore it on your own or on guided tours leaving from the Hosting Center. Among the points of interest are several museums (Life Sciences, Earth Sciences, Peoples and Cultures and a Fine Arts Center). The **Marriott Activities Center** is a modern indoor arena, one of the largest in the nation, with events of all types being held. Check locally for the current schedule. The football stadium seats 60,000. Expect to spend at least an hour touring the campus, whether on your own or with the student guide service.

When we depart Provo it will be via a highly scenic route known as the **Alpine Scenic Loop Road**, consisting of a section of US 189 and UT 92. The loop leads back to I-15 and covers about 40 miles. This is double the distance of heading straight up I-15, but the extra 20 miles is more than worth it. Head out of Provo via University Avenue, the primary north-south artery in town, which also happens to be US 189. Four miles north of the city, shortly after entering attractive Provo Canyon you'll come to **Bridal Veil Falls**. The Falls drop more than 600 feet in two cascades. The view is great from the bottom, but even better if you take the aerial tramway to the top. It goes up over 1,200 feet and is one of the steepest such rides in the world. From the top there are excellent views of Utah

Valley. The round trip to the top, including viewing time, will take 45 minutes to an hour.

Another eight miles on US 189 will bring you to the cutoff for UT 92, as the Alpine Scenic Loop continues. You'll pass the Sundance Resort, owned by Robert Redford, a beautiful place that offers recreational and cultural activities in a setting par excellence.

The loop road is narrow and very twisting but isn't all that difficult to negotiate. The entire route is dominated by views of 11,750-foot Mt. Timpanogos, which rises over 7,000 feet higher than the Utah Valley. There are many trails but most are long and require considerable effort. Allow about 90 minutes for the driving portion of the Alpine Scenic Loop.

One other attraction needs mentioning. **Timpanogos Cave National Monument** is a series of three interconnected caves with fantastic and beautiful formations. Man-made tunnels join them. There are guided tours lasting about an hour. The problem is that the cave is located about a thousand feet above the loop road. It is reached by a 1 1/2-mile trail (each way). Given the gain in elevation and the high altitudes, it is a difficult climb that should not be attempted unless you're in very good physical condition. If you're going to do it, allow about three hours or more for the round-trip hike and cave tour. Tours are limited to 20 people so it fills up fast. Advance ticket purchase is strongly recommended.

UT 72 will bring you back to the Interstate where we'll resume traveling northbound, but just for 14 miles to Exit 301. Then proceed on UT 48, also known as the Bingham Highway, for nine miles to the end and follow the signs to **Kennecott Utah Company's Bingham Canyon Copper Mine.** This extraordinary place is the world's largest open pit mine and excavating operations go on continuously. It was originally developed to mine gold and silver but copper has been the only product since early in the century. The statistics are amazing: the terraced slopes of the pit measure about 2 1/2 miles across and over 2,500 feet deep. This translates into a mining area encompassing more than 1,900 acres. It's easy to understand how something this size could yield over 12 million tons of copper and still be going strong!

In a state known for its scenic wonders, this man-made hole in the ground has a unique beauty of its own, bringing out the same kind of awe as does a great canyon. You know it's big but you don't fully comprehend it until you focus on one of the mammoth dump trucks, far larger than any on-road vehicle you've ever encountered; here they look like little toys making their way up and down the terraced slopes.

Return to Interstate 15 the opposite way that you came in and head north one final time. You'll be back in Salt Lake City in a matter of minutes. If you're going to be doing some city sightseeing, then it's best to take I-15 to Exit 310 which will leave you practically in the heart of downtown on 600 Street South. On the other hand, if you're heading for the airport, stay on I-15 for only one exit, pick up I-215 north and you'll be at your destination in 14 miles.

Alternative Routes

As was the case with Colorado, the suggested itinerary that we've just followed covered the major portion of the state and hit many of its noteworthy attractions. This doesn't mean that there isn't more to see. Utah's sights are almost unlimited; time is the main obstacle. Many of the places that follow can be seen as short additions to or substitutions for part of the main itinerary, except for the two sections called WEST INTO THE DESERT and ON THE TRAIL OF THE DINOSAURS. Everything else that follows is close to the main route. For your convenience we will deal first with destinations reached from Salt Lake City, then with attractions elsewhere in the state.

A LOOP EXCURSION FROM SALT LAKE CITY: This loop covers about 150 miles and can be traversed in one long day, but it's better as an overnight trip. Another option is to break it into two parts and use Salt Lake City as a base. It covers the territory east and north of the capital; the nearby attractions to the west are described in the subsequent section.

As mentioned earlier, Salt Lake City's eastern border touches on the **Wasatch Mountain range**. Wasatch is an Indian word meaning "mountain pass" and it's very appropriate because this beautiful range is penetrated by many canyons.

Among the most popular are **City Creek Canyon**, which begins across the street from the east side of the State Capitol; **Big Cottonwood** (UT 152), starting at the east end of 7000 South Street; **Little**

Cottonwood Canyon (UT 210), which branches off of Big Cottonwood Canyon; and **Mill Creek Canyon**, entered via 3900 South Street. All four provide magnificent scenery and (except for City Creek Canyon) have picnic and other recreational areas for drop-in visitors. Trails in all of the canyons climb the Wasatch and provide great views of the Salt Valley. Big Cottonwood ends at the resort of Brighton while its little sister leads to the Alta and Snowbird resort areas. While all of these resorts are best known as winter skiing destinations, they are places of tranquil beauty at any time of the year.

Our loop route leaves Salt Lake via Interstate 80 eastbound from downtown and passes through a canyon too. **Parleys Canyon** is just as scenic as the others, although a bit more difficult to appreciate because you'll be traveling at fast Interstate speeds. The road climbs to an altitude well over 6,000 feet less than 10 miles from downtown.

It's approximately 20 miles on I-80 to Exit 145 (UT 224), and then six miles south on that road to Park City. This former mining town from days gone by has now evolved into one of the state's biggest resorts instead of becoming a ghost town like so many other mining communities throughout the west. It combines modern resorts of all kinds with historic buildings from the 19th and early 20th centuries. The town's past is best explored in the **Park City Museum** at 528 Main Street. Besides the usual pictures and artifacts, the museum has a restored jail. The community's Visitor Center is also here and the staff can help you with a walking tour of the historic district. Park City has the usual motel accommodations but there are also a number of luxury resorts or you can stay at one of the many condominiums that are semi hotels or have time sharing.

After you've finished touring Park City, go back to I-80 and continue east for another 23 miles to where the road splits with Interstate 84. Take I-84 approximately nine miles to a marked viewing area for the **Devil's Slide**. This landmark rock has the shape of a slide seen in a playground. It must have been used during the Jolly Green Giant's childhood.

Continue on I-84 to Exit 87, which is US 89. A short ride of six miles north will bring you into Ogden, the state's third largest city. US 89 becomes Washington Boulevard, which is the main thoroughfare in Ogden. Stay on this street until you get to 25th Street and then make a left. In three blocks you will reach Union Station. Dating from 1924 this massive structure used to be one of the west's busiest railroad stations. Most of it now has been turned into the **Union Station Museums**, an interesting collection covering a wide range of subjects. But first step into the huge central lobby and take a look at two murals that depict railroad history in Utah. As would be expected, one of the many museums here is a railroad museum. There is also a car museum that has rotating exhibits of automobiles as well as a small permanent collection of antique classics in perfect condition. One of the best museums here is the firearms museum. It concentrates on the Browning family of firearms. A natural history museum and an art gallery complete the picture. It should take you at least two hours to go through all of the museums. Ogden's Visitor Center is also located in the station complex.

Like Salt Lake City, Ogden has a Temple Square with Mormon Temple and Tabernacle. You may want to take a quick look, but the attractive complex doesn't equal Salt Lake's.

Take 24th Street west across the railroad tracks to **Fort Buenaventura State Park**. This is a recreated trading post from the mid-1840s and a brief visit here will give you a good idea of how the traders of this mountain region lived. Allow 30 minutes. From here there is access to Interstate 15.

Just a few miles south of downtown (Exit 341) is the huge Hill Air Force Base. Near the Interstate exit follow signs for the **Hill Aerospace Museum**. The Museum has a collection of vintage and modern aircraft, with emphasis on military applications, plus engines and other exhibits. One of the highlights is a flight simulator. Allow 30-45 minutes.

The Ogden area has many accommodations but, since it's only 30 miles on I-15 back to Salt Lake City, you probably won't want to stay here.

One diversion between Ogden and Salt Lake City that might interest you, especially if you have children along, is the **Lagoon Amusement Park** in Farmington at Exit 326. Here you'll find a recreation of a frontier town where you can take a train ride or a stagecoach ride. There is also western entertainment in a stadium and musicals are held in the **Opera House**. It's educational but entertaining and provides a break for children. Admission is expensive, however, so unless you plan to spend at least a few hours here it may not be worth the price.

WEST INTO THE DESERT: This excursion travels due west from Salt Lake City on or adjacent to I-80 for a one-way distance of 125 miles to the town of Wendover on the Utah-Nevada border. There are plenty of places to stay in Wendover; those on the Nevada side of town even have casinos or at least slot machines.

To the immediate west of Salt Lake City is the **Great Salt Lake**. This body of water is over 70 miles by 30 miles wide and is far saltier than the ocean. In fact, only the Dead Sea has a higher salt content. Despite the briny water there is one type of fish that has taken hold. The primary life form is algae, which sometimes gives the water a blue-green or even reddish tint. The depth of the lake has varied considerably over time but now averages well under 30 feet. The Great Salt Lake is the remnant of a much larger ancient freshwater lake. It's a popular place to swim because the salt makes it so buoyant that people float easily. Be careful, though, not to get the water in your eyes, nose or throat because it can be quite irritating.

The lake contains several islands, the largest one being Antelope, a narrow, 15-mile-long island with a mountain peak rising to almost 6,600 feet. A newly opened causeway has replaced an earlier one that became submerged in the early 1980s. It leads to **Antelope Island State Park** where you will encounter marshes, dunes, mountains and wildlife. Allow about an hour to explore the park.

A number of beaches dot the southern shore of the lake at **Great Salt Lake State Park**. There is a Visitor Center in the park which tells about the fascinating and often turbulent history of the lake. Many visitors are surprised to learn about the constant ebb and flow of its shores, including the time when a major resort built here in the early 1900s was swallowed up by the lake. There has been a lot of talk about rebuilding it. Access to the lake is best from Exit 111 off I-80, then by the frontage road.

Continuing west on I-80 you soon enter the desert. At first the high mountain peaks, some more than 12,000 feet, seem too numerous to count. But the area is classified as a desert nonetheless, based on the fact that less than 10 inches of rain falls here in a year. The mountains, although never out of view, eventually give way to the Salt Flats. By the time you near Wendover, it'll look more like what you expect a desert should be. In the town of Wendover (on Wendover Boulevard, running parallel to I-80) is the **Bonneville Speedway Museum**, The museum collection ranges from classic cars to those that have gone more than 600 miles per hour on the speedway. After seeing the museum you'll want to head out to the **Bonneville Salt Flats International Speedway**; take Exit 4 and follow the signs. Speed Week (the third week of August) brings a lot of visitors for the races but at other times it is generally quiet. The enormous speedway tract covers more than 700,000 acres. At most times the ground is covered by a thin layer of water, but in the summer the water is completely absorbed, leaving a salty, hard white surface. You are allowed to drive on the Salt Flats and perhaps imagine that you're roaring along in a test vehicle at hundreds of miles per hour. But be sure to remain only in marked areas; other sections may not be able to sustain the weight of your car. Getting stuck out here in the blistering desert sun would definitely not be a pleasant experience.

This unique area is fascinating but the 250-mile round trip may not be worthwhile if you do not have a fascination for the desolate desert environment. If you're coming from northern California, however, you'll be traveling right by here on your way into Utah, so it will certainly be worth seeing.

ON THE TRAIL OF THE DINOSAURS: This route covers a round-trip distance of just under 500 miles and requires three days or more to complete. The route travels into the remote northeastern corner of the state where you'll encounter long stretches of un-spoiled wilderness. Begin by leaving Salt Lake City on Interstate 80 eastbound to Exit 148 and pick up US 40 for 19 miles to Heber City. This attractive town is surrounded by Alpine scenery. The **Heber Valley Historic Railroad** (once known as the "Heber Creeper") travels into Provo Canyon. The trip takes about three hours but is worthwhile if you will not be doing the section of the main itinerary that includes Provo Canyon and that comes from the opposite direction. Despite the high altitude you'll see a lot of farms and agricultural activity in the vicinity of Heber.

US 40 is a pleasantly scenic drive with plenty of mountains and a number of beautiful lakes and reservoirs, including **Strawberry Reservoir**, about 20 miles past Heber City. There is good fishing here if you want to spend some quiet time. About 70 miles from Heber City, US 40 is joined by US 191 at the town of Duchesne. The road continues through a series of mountain ranges (but the driving is easy) and through or past several sections of the Uintah and Ouray Indian Reservation. About 3,000 Ute Indians live here. Do not stray from the road onto the reservation unless you have received permission to do so.

From Duchesne, where you can get gas and food, it's almost 60 miles to Vernal, largest town in this part of the state. You can make a base here for excursions to the nearby major attractions. Accommodations can be found in several good motels, including a couple of **Best Westerns.**

In town is the **Pioneer Museum** (200 South and 550 West), a local history exhibit, but the biggest attraction is the **Utah Field House of Natural History** on East Main Street. Well before *Jurassic Park*, this museum was educating and thrilling visitors of all ages. The outdoor dinosaur garden has many full-sized and menacingly real looking dinosaur models in a setting that would be considered "natural" if you'd been around a couple of million years ago. A swamp area is especially interesting. Indoor exhibits include fossils of insects and animals both small and large, as well as some exceptionally large examples of real dinosaur bones. Indian history and mounted specimens of wildlife found throughout Utah complete the museum. Allow about 90 minutes to fully explore this first-class facility.

The museum is a good introduction to the real thing, the **Dinosaur National Monument.** Located 13 miles east of Vernal via US 40 and then six miles north on UT 149, this straddles the northern part of the Green River. Most of the acreage lies in Colorado, but the dinosaur quarry is in Utah. More dinosaur remains have been found here than anywhere else in the country. A spiral ramp brings you slowly up to an observation deck from where you can look out onto the quarry, which has been left as it appeared during the time when most excavations were taking place. Exhibits explain the reasons why dinosaur bones were well preserved in this area and tell much about the archaeological work that has occurred and is still going on. In fact, you can look through windows into a paleontology lab and see scientists doing their thing.

Dinosaur National Monument has more to see than fossils and bones. It's in a very scenic area of canyons and mountains, some rising more than 4,000 feet above the Green River. Although the Utah part of the monument is scenic, it's even more so in the Colorado portion. If you want to get there you have to go back outside the monument and six miles north on UT 149, this straddles the northern part of the Green River. The dinosaur quarry is ery, but especially the segment that passes through the Little Colorado River Gorge. This narrow and deep gorge will at least put the

Grand Canyon out of your mind for the moment. There are several outstanding viewpoints where you can stop.

The remainder of the attractions on this route all lie to the north of Vernal and are reached by US 191. The 35 miles from Vernal to the junction of UT 44 are known as the **Drive Through the Ages** because of the many geologic formations from a variety of eras that can be seen along the way. Much of the route lies within the very scenic Ashley National Forest. You can pick up a brochure at the Vernal Welcome Center (at the Utah Field House) that describes the different formations and gives you their exact location along the drive. You'll want to stop at some of the points of interest so give yourself more than an hour to complete the drive.

Ten miles north of Vernal and then two miles east following signs is the **Red Fleet State Park**. The main feature is three red sandstone cliffs that are shaped somewhat like ships, hence the name. It's a brief stop but a very beautiful one.

At the junction of US 191 and UT 44 you will be entering the vast **Flaming Gorge National Recreation Area**. This huge area extends across Utah's northern border into Wyoming. Although the bigger portion of the Recreation Area lies within Wyoming, most of the facilities as well as the best scenery are located on the Utah side of the border. Flaming Gorge is within the high Uinta Mountains and contains more than 90 miles of reservoirs in magnificent fire-red canyons that give the area its name. The deep, bright red is enhanced by the seemingly ever-present sunshine.

We'll first consider the attractions along UT 44 (left at the junction when coming up US 191 from Vernal), which stretches for 34 miles along the southeastern fringe of Flaming Gorge.

Three miles into UT 44 is the **Red Canyon Visitor Center**. From here you look down a sheer drop of approximately 1,400 feet onto the deep blue lake from a series of viewpoints connected by an easy nature trail. Another two miles further down the road will bring you to the **Jones Hole National Fish Hatchery**. Besides the hatchery operations, which are interesting if you have never seen one before, there is a trail that penetrates a stunning canyon hemmed in by 2,000 foot high walls. Then proceed to a cutoff on UT 44 for **Sheep Creek Canyon**. This is a 13-mile loop that will bring you back to UT 44 a bit south of the town of Manila (where food is available). The road through Sheep Creek Canyon is narrow but paved and is a haven for those who are interested in fossils. Even if you aren't particularly interest in that aspect of the canyon, the scenery is enough to please just about anyone. Then head back down to the junction with US 191 and take the latter road north. Just south of the town of Dutch John (food and lodging available if you aren't staying in Vernal) is the **Flaming Gorge Dam and Visitor Center**. The dam is 500 feet high and about 1,300 feet long at the top. Both guided and self-guided tours are available (lasting about 30 minutes). You go down to the powerhouse and learn about the operation of the dam. Additional exhibits are located in the Visitor Center. This area also has outstanding vistas of Flaming Gorge, some of the best being from right along the top of the dam.

Flaming Gorge also has all kinds of water sports. You can rent boats of many types in several locations. Expect to spend at least a half-day in Flaming Gorge National Recreation Area. It makes an excellent full-day outing from Vernal.

The suggested way back to Salt Lake City is in the opposite direction from the trip in. If, however, you are not going to be linking up with the suggested main itinerary it's possible to go back by a different route – do the US 191 portion of Flaming Gorge first, then after completing the UT 44 section continue into Wyoming and take WY 414 to I-80 westbound. You don't save any significant mileage and the scenery is generally not as good as going back by US 40, but it's different and will take less time since a larger portion of the route is on the Interstate.

On the other hand, if you're going to be doing all or part of the main itinerary, head back on US 40/US 191 to Duchesne. At that point stay on US 191 when the two routes split. A scenic 45-mile section of US 191 brings you to the town of Helper and the main route. Doing it this way adds about 350 miles to the main route instead of the 500 required by going all the way back to Salt Lake City.

OTHER SIDE TRIPS: Each of the mini-trips contained in this part are spurs or loops off of the main route. Individually they don't add that much time or mileage but keep in mind that doing all of them will begin to add up quickly. So you'll want to pick and choose.

Our first side trip explores the beautiful La Sal Mountains via the **La Sal Mountains Loop Road** to the east of the canyon country. Moab, which provided a good base for touring Arches and Canyonlands is also the starting and ending point for this loop, which only tacks on an additional 45 miles to your trip. A few words about the La Sal Mountains are in order. The La Sals are the second highest group of mountains in Utah, with about a half-dozen peaks exceeding 12,000 feet. There is a greater variety of wildlife because the temperature is not so hot at these altitudes as in the canyon country. Except for Moab there aren't any towns of significance. There may actually be more ghost towns from the mining days than there are still active communities.

The entire road is paved, but many short spurs leading from it are gravel or dirt and are made even more difficult by the steep grades. As they are often impassable except for high-clearance four-wheel drive vehicles, we'll confine ourselves to the main road, which has more than enough scenery to satisfy those taking this excursion.

The loop begins eight miles south of Moab. Rising steadily through several climatic zones, you'll come to an overlook in about 20 miles. There is a dramatic view of the Castle Valley and you can see all the way into the interior of Arches National Park. In another ten miles you'll reach a view of Round Mountain, a large formation of volcanic origin that rises prominently from the surrounding valley. Soon after that are a series of rock spires, including the oddly named Priest and Nuns.

The La Sal Mountains Loop Road ends at UT 128 (described in the main itinerary) and from this point it's only 17 miles west of Moab. You should plan on the loop taking at least three hours to complete.

Our next excursion is not too far from the La Sal Road. It covers a round trip distance of exactly 100 miles, via UT 211. This road branches off of US 191 about 40 miles south of Moab. About 12 miles into the route is the **Newspaper Rock State Historic Monu-ment**. An easy trail along red sandstone rocks reveals many re-markably well preserved Indian petroglyphs. They cover almost 2,000 years of Indian culture, from before the Anasazi tribes through the Navajo. Among the figures painted here are humans, animals and birds and several abstract representations. A short nature trail will acquaint you with the desert vegetation.

UT 211 ends where the pavement does, at the **Needles Overlook** in the southern portion of Canyonlands National Park. You peer down at a sheer drop of about a thousand feet, a dramatic enough sight by itself. But, looking out ahead from here, you can see almost all of Canyonlands. The most spectacular view is toward the Needles, rocky spires numbering in the thousands, like a city from another planet. From this point you can also see where the Green and Colorado Rivers meet as well as a good portion of the almost impassable Maze District.

Other roads in the area lead to equally impressive views and trails but they are unpaved and mostly difficult. Retrace the drive on UT 211 back to US 189. This side trip can easily be done in less than three hours.

The third side trip is in Color Country, beginning at the town of Mt. Carmel Junction. Before doing the Zion-Mt. Carmel Highway (UT 9), remain on US 89 southbound. It is 17 miles from there to the town of Kanab on a good road traversing a scenic summit at 6,650 feet. This area is known for the **Vermillion Cliffs** (another portion of which can be seen on a side trip in the Arizona chapter). Every turn in the road will produce a different view of these colorful formations, with the angle of the sun relative to your position determining the shading. At times (most pronounced at sunrise and sunset) the cliffs seem to be aglow. In the town of Kanab, population 3,500, are a couple of interesting attractions. The first is **Frontier Movie Town** (located on West Center Street), with an Old West motif. It has been used in a number of movies and television shows. **Moqui Cave** is five miles north of town on US 89. This relatively small and delightfully cool cave contains Indian artifacts (placed there by the owners), along with fossils and minerals. Especially noteworthy is the fluorescent mineral collection. This attraction doesn't take long at all, but you should allocate about an hour for the Movie Town.

Eight miles north of Kanab and then left following signs for about ten miles is the **Coral Pink Sand Dunes State Park**. The sand dunes often reach several hundred feet high and are given their pink color by quartz particles mixed into the sand – it has nothing to do with coral. Be advised that only off-road vehicles are allowed to ride on the dunes.

This entire side trip covers only about 40 miles and can be done, including all attractions, in less than four hours. However, it can be extended a great deal with one of two alternatives.

If you stay on US 89 past Kanab it is 75 miles one way to the town of Page, Arizona (a few miles over the Utah line) and access to **Glen**

Canyon National Recreation Area and **Rainbow Bridge National Monument**. These attractions are covered in full in the Arizona chapter but if you're not going to be doing that trip you might want to consider adding them as an alternative route here. At least one full day is required for the attractions and the round-trip of 150 miles.

The other alternative is to take US 89A (Alternative 89) from Kanab for a distance of 80 miles south to the **North Rim of Grand Canyon National Park**. This, again, is included in the Arizona chapter. This extension will also require the addition of at least one full day.

The final side trip for Utah can be either an extension of the previously discussed loop from Salt Lake City, or a trip in itself from Salt Lake on the main itinerary. Either way, take Interstate 15 north to the Brigham City exit, number 364. However, if you are coming during the summer get off at the town of Willard, Exit 360, and head into Brigham City via Old Highway 89, known as the **Golden Spike Fruitway**. Orchards of cherries, peaches, apricots and other fruits and vegetables line the road for miles. And in summer the growers set up fruit stands along the road. Delicious and refreshing fruit at bargain prices is well worth the detour from the Interstate. It's also very colorful.

Brigham City is named for Brigham Young and was previously called Box Elder. The **Box Elder Tabernacle** on Main Street is almost a hundred years old. This Gothic-style building is considered by many visitors and locals alike to be one of the most beautiful structures in the state. Tours are available.

The ride to **Inspiration Point** is listed here only for the more adventurous visitors. Main Street in the adjacent town of Mantua (reached by US 91) is the beginning of a 28-mile round trip to 9,422-foot-high Inspiration Point. From the top you'll have not only views of the Great Salt Lake and much of northern Utah, but three other states (Nevada, Idaho and Wyoming). While the view certainly ranks with the best found anywhere, the trip is on a narrow, twisting and steep road which could be hazardous for drivers not experienced with mountain roads. Allow at least 90 minutes for the round trip.

The **Golden Spike National Historic Site** is not too far from Brigham City, and is reached by a 30-mile drive from I-15's Exit 368 along UT 83. This site describes in detail the fascinating develments that led up to selection of this remote place in the Promontory Mountains as the point where the Central Pacific and Union Pacific would join together to forge the first transcontinental railroad. The extensive Visitor Center also has exhibits on the construction of the railroad and the linkage that occurred on May 10, 1869 – a momentous occasion that forever changed the face of the American west.

Don't expect to see railroads running through here today. A cutoff built in the early 1900s eliminated the need for trains to make the twisting and steep climb through the Promontory. But fret not. Replicas of the two historic locomotives that met here are on a small rebuilt section of track and give you an idea of what took place on the actual meeting day.

The site is in an area of great scenic beauty as well. Take the **East Promontory Auto Trail** to the end and them embark on the **Big Fill Walk**. This 1 1/2-mile trail will take you through rugged terrain and give you an idea of the problems that were faced in building the railroads. A number of ravines that had to be crossed are seen on the walk.

Including the Visitor Center and exhibits, along with the auto trail and Big Fill Walk, your visit to Golden Spike will last a minimum of two hours. You can return to Salt Lake City via UT 83 and I-15, a total distance of only 90 miles.

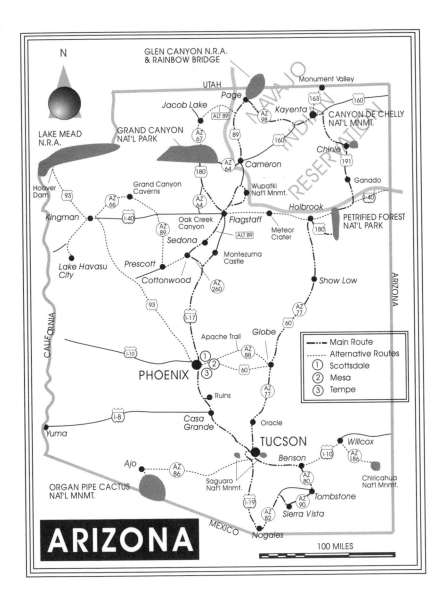

Chapter 3

Arizona: Nature's Splendor

Tell anyone that you're going to Arizona and visions of the Grand Canyon will appear before their eyes. But Arizona, sixth largest of the states, has so much diversity that after spending a week or two exploring its many facets the Grand Canyon, fabulous as it may be, will be just one of many wonderful memories.

Besides its well known canyon, Arizona is a land of beautiful multi-colored deserts, dense forests, rugged mountain ranges, vast plateaus and incredible rock formations. Add to that an equally diverse mixture of cultures (no other state has more Native Americans), year-round sunshine without humidity, and almost unlimited recreational opportunities, and it becomes easy to understand the popularity of Arizona as a tourist destination and as an ideal place for retirement.

One important practical note before we begin our tour. Although all three states in this book are in the Mountain Time Zone, Arizona does not participate in Daylight Savings Time. Therefore, from April through October, Arizona is on Mountain Standard Time, which is one hour earlier than in either Colorado or Utah. Confusing, isn't it? One trick is to forget about Standard and Daylight Savings times and remember that Arizona is on the equivalent of Pacific Time during the summer. (An exception to all of this is the Navajo Indian Reservation in the northwest corner of the state — they change time with the rest of us!)

Along the Suggested Itinerary

As was the case in both Colorado and Utah, we'll begin our journey in the state capital because it provides the easiest access by air from the rest of the nation. However, due to Phoenix's location it is not the place to begin if you are driving into Arizona (except for those coming in from southern California via I-10). Other visitors will likely enter Arizona from the east on I-40 and can pick up the main itinerary at Chambers (Exit 133). Many other connection points are also available.

Sky Harbor International Airport is only four miles from downtown Phoenix, making it one of the most conveniently located airports of any major city in the country. The access road leads directly onto the city's excellent highway system. Follow signs for I-10 West/I-17 North (they run together through the southern part of Phoenix as the Maricopa Freeway). Take Exit 195B (7th Street) and you're already downtown.

The layout of streets in Phoenix is an easy and orderly grid pattern with few exceptions and applies to the entire city, not just the downtown business core. Numbered streets run from north to south and named streets travel east to west. Central Avenue is the primary north/south axis. Numbered streets (1st Street, 2nd Street, etc.) work their way upward from east of Central, while numbered avenues head west of Central. For example, 5th Street is five blocks east of Central Avenue and 5th Avenue is five blocks west. A North or South prefix to the numbered streets and avenues depends upon whether you find yourself north or south of Washington Street, an important east/west thoroughfare that runs through downtown. Likewise, named streets have an East or West designation in relation to which side of Central Avenue they lie on. Controlled access highways that lead to all parts of the city and surrounding suburbs are I-10, I-17, AR 51 and US 60.

The Phoenix and Valley of the Sun Convention and Visitors Bureau is in the Hyatt Regency Hotel at 122 N. 2nd Street. You can get information about your visit here and its central location also makes it a good point to start a downtown walking tour.

Two blocks south of the Visitors Bureau is the **Civic Plaza**. It's worth a brief stroll through this attractive modern development that houses the imposing Symphony Hall as well as the Convention Center and other public buildings. The broad central plaza has some interesting sculptures. Across the street from the 2nd Street side of the Plaza at Washington Street is the **Arizona Museum of Science and Technology**. It seems that every major city has to have one of these facilities, but this one is a notch above most in its

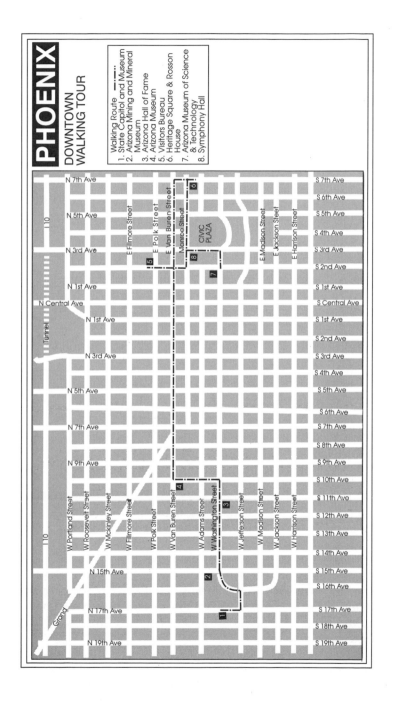

PHOENIX

DOWNTOWN
WALKING TOUR

Walking Route ‑‑‑‑‑
1. State Capitol and Museum
2. Arizona Mining and Mineral
   Museum
3. Arizona Hall of Fame
4. Arizona Museum
5. Visitors Bureau
6. Heritage Square & Rosson
   House
7. Arizona Museum of Science
   & Technology
8. Symphony Hall

appeal as virtually all of the exhibits are interactive. You'll hardly notice an hour or more passing by.

Now go back across Civic Plaza to the east until you reach 6th Street. Turn left and at the intersection of Monroe (notice that downtown streets all bear the names of American Presidents), **Heritage Square** is a small area of restored structures from the latter part of the 19th Century. An attractive small garden is on the premises but the highlights are the **Arizona Doll and Toy Museum** (in Stevens House), which contains dolls from all over the world dating back as far as the 1700s, and the **Rosson House**, former home of Phoenix's mayor just before the turn of the century. The elaborate Victorian mansion is noted for its exceptionally rich wood working. You should plan on the entire Heritage Square complex taking about 90 minutes to complete.

One block north of the Square is Van Buren Street. Turn left and proceed to 10th Avenue. This is a lengthy walk (1 1/4 miles), especially if you're under a typical blazing Phoenix sun, so you might want to hop a bus on Van Buren. Either way you'll soon reach the **Arizona Museum**, a small but very interesting place that chronicles more than 20 centuries of Arizona history, from ancient Indian cultures right into our century. Allow about 30 minutes. Only three blocks away at Washington and 11th Avenue is the **Arizona Hall of Fame**. The classic-style building in which the collection is housed once served as a public library. Now the exhibits deal with the men and women who have made important contributions to the development of Arizona. Even some of Arizona's notorious villains are included. You should be able to see the museum in about a half-hour.

Four blocks west at 15th Street is the **Arizona Mining and Mineral Museum**. (Does anything around here begin with a word other than Arizona? Yes, but have a little patience.) While Arizona has had its share of gold and silver mining, the state is a treasure trove of beautiful gemstones of every variety. They're all on display here, some in special fluorescent-lit rooms that display the phosphorescent qualities of the minerals. Exhibits on gem cutting and polishing round out the displays. It will take about 45 minutes to explore this fascinating collection.

To the west of the Mining Museum, Washington Street curves into Jefferson. Turn right at that point and walk for one block until you reach the park-like grounds of the State Capitol. The **Arizona State**

Capitol Museum was built in 1900 as the territorial capitol before Arizona achieved statehood in 1912. Exhibits display historic artifacts and documents. Several offices, including that of the governor, have been restored to their original appearance. The adjacent current state capitol is a modern structure built in the 1970s and although the legislative galleries are open to the public, the building is of no special interest.

That wraps up the central downtown area, although there are some other attractions not too far from this area. However, it would be best to get to them by car or bus. Phoenix Transit will tell you how to get from one place to another – call (602) 253-5000. Bus information is also available at the Visitors' Bureau. The **Phoenix Art Museum** is about half a mile north of downtown at N. Central Avenue and McDowell Road. While there is a good selection of both western American and Mexican art, the museum is best known for its collection of Medieval and Renaissance works and an excellent Oriental gallery. While many people will be able to visit the museum in well under an hour, art lovers and connoisseurs will require a considerably longer time. Still on Central Avenue, but several blocks north at Monte Vista Road, is the outstanding **Heard Museum**. This is arguably the most comprehensive collection anywhere on the history and culture of Native Americans. Although the museum concentrates on the tribes of the American southwest, the entire western hemisphere is well represented. The exhibits and artifacts are both extensive and informative. Accordingly, allow between 60 and 90 minutes for anything more than a casual visit.

If you haven't gotten back into your car up to this point you'll have to do so now because we're going to be exploring some interesting attractions in the southern and eastern parts of Phoenix. Drive south on 7th Street all the way to its end where you'll bump into the **Mystery Castle**. It was built by an eccentric individual named Boyce Gulley in the 1930s. Although it looks like a castle, it was not built with ordinary construction materials – in addition to native Arizona stone, Mr. Gulley used just about anything he could get his hands on. The interior is equally eclectic, combining both Indian artifacts and antiques (some would say "junk") of every conceivable nature. Guided tours last about half an hour.

From the Castle go a block north to Dobbins Road, turn left for one block to Central Avenue and make another left. This will lead you into the huge **South Mountain Park**. At almost 17,000 acres, it is claimed to be the world's largest city park. There is a paved road that leads to Dobbins Lookout. At an elevation of 2,330 feet, it is approximately 1,200 feet above Phoenix, and provides spectacular views of the city as well as the mountains north of Phoenix. While the mountains surrounding Phoenix are not as dramatic as those near Denver or Salt Lake City, the contrast between them and the flat Valley of the Sun is still impressive. Besides the view from the mountain top, South Mountain Park has interesting rock formations and a variety of cacti and shrubs unique to the area. Numerous hiking trails and picnic areas are scattered throughout the park. The roads leading through the park and up to the summit are narrow and winding, so exercise caution. While 30 to 45 minutes is long enough to get to the top, take in the view, and get back down to the city, allow longer if you plan to try out any of the trails or other recreational opportunities in the park. (The north side of town has another park, appropriately called **North Mountain Park**, that is a lot smaller but similar in nature to South Mountain. You might want to consider doing that one instead if you are pressed for time and are heading out of Phoenix to the north.)

From South Mountain take Central Avenue north for about a mile to Baseline Road. Turn right and proceed as far as 48th Street, then head north until Washington Street and go east two blocks to the **Pueblo Grande Museum**. This archaeological site is a reconstruction of a Hohokam Indian site that, for reasons unknown, disappeared around the 15th century. A museum building contains artifacts that were uncovered at the site, but the most interesting part of your visit will be the short trail that leads to a ceremonial mound constructed in the 12th century. The mound overlooks the Salt River and you get a great view of the remains of canals that were constructed by the Hohokam. Allow 45 minutes to an hour for your visit.

A short distance east (at Van Buren and 61st Street) is the **Hall of Flame Museum of Firefighting**. One of the largest museums of its type, the Hall of Flame contains several galleries devoted to different areas of firefighting history. These include hand pumpers from as far back as the early 1700s, motorized firefighting equipment, fire alarm systems and fire safety. This is an educational experience for all ages that can be covered in about 45 minutes.

Near to the Hall of Flame, branch off of Van Buren onto Galvin Parkway and proceed north for about one mile to the **Phoenix Zoo**. This hilly site of more than 100 acres contains well over a thousand animals, many native to Arizona but also those native to tropical regions from all different parts of the world. You can walk around the grounds or take a "Safari-Train" at a slight extra cost. In either case allow a minimum of 90 minutes and, as we have said before, more if you have children with you. We should also mention the **Wildlife World Zoo** which is located in the northern portion of Phoenix. This is a smaller zoo that began as a place to house endangered species. It still specializes in rare animals as compared to the Phoenix Zoo. While you probably won't want to see both unless you're really into captive wildlife, consider Wildlife World instead of the regular Zoo if more exotic animals are your preference.

Finally, just north of the Zoo is the beautiful **Desert Botanical Garden**. A 1 1/2-mile trail winds through the garden and passes some 2,000 species of cacti and other forms of desert vegetation on this 150-acre site. The very best time to visit is in the spring when the gorgeous cactus flowers are in bloom. Allocate between 45 minutes and an hour for your visit.

Before we proceed to the numerous attractions of suburban Phoenix, we want to digress for a moment and talk about the weather. If you are coming in summer it is an understatement to call it "hot." People tell you it's dry, but so is an oven! Although we have arranged the touring in a convenient manner from a geographic standpoint, you may wish to use the cooler mornings for outdoor attractions and spend the afternoon inside air conditioned museums, especially if you are easily fatigued by the heat.

THE SUBURBS: The adjacent communities of Tempe, Mesa and Scottsdale all lie to the east of Phoenix and, together, have a population of over half a million people and enough attractions to consume a lot of good sightseeing time. Both Tempe and Mesa can be reached easily from Phoenix via US 60 (the Superstition Freeway) or by continuing east on Van Buren Street, which becomes Apache Boulevard once reaching Tempe.

Tempe is the home of **Arizona State University**, a lovely campus covering more than 600 acres and filled with palm trees. Among the many cultural attractions here are the **Nelson Fine Arts Museum** and **Matthews Center** (both part of the University Art Museum), and several smaller museums devoted to anthropology, geology, zoology and various other arts and sciences. It would take many hours to do all of them, so you're better off picking out the

topics that interest you most and allowing about an hour or so to
do them.

Continuing on Apache Blvd. from Tempe, it isn't far to Mesa where
the first two attractions are within blocks of each other on Apache.
The **Mesa Southwest Museum** is another museum of local history
and culture but with a number of interesting features. There is a
recreation of an Indian cave dwelling, petroglyphs,, a frontier jail
that you can try to break out of and a visit to the Dutchman's
Treasure Mine. Allow close to an hour for your visit. The **Arizona
Temple Visitor Center** is on the grounds of the Mesa Mormon
Temple and, like those in Utah, the temple itself is off limits to
non-Mormons. However, even if you visited temples in Utah this
is worth a brief stop because the grounds are probably the most
beautiful of any Mormon temple. There is exotic desert vegetation
and the landscaping enhances the beauty of the temple itself − a
structure in the classic Greek style. Visitor Center tours are available.

From the Temple proceed north on Mesa Drive to the **Crimson
Farms & Heritage Museum** at the intersection of N. Horne Street.
The museum describes the achievements of the pioneers who
settled Mesa but is especially strong in its collection of farm equipment and implements. Southwestern history is depicted in a series
of murals. Allow about 45 minutes. Five miles to the east at Falcon
Field is the **Champlin Fighter Museum**, which displays memora-
bilia from pilots who served in combat dating back to the First
World War. Also on display are fighter aircraft from America, its
allies and enemies. Allow at least a half-hour. Just south of the
museum is McKellips Road. Head west (right turn) and once you
cross over the Salt River you'll be in Scottsdale.

This attractive community features western architecture (porch-
fronted shopping areas) as well as Spanish-style adobe buildings.
In the center of town is the very attractive **Scottsdale Civic Center
and Mall**, a municipal complex that also houses an art center.
You'll wish that the town you live in had an area as nice as this!
Scottsdale's other attractions are mostly located north of the center
of town, all accessible from Scottsdale Road. The first is the **Cosanti
Foundation**, five miles north on Doubletree Ranch Road. A scale
model of architect Paolo Soleri's prototype city of **Arcosanti** is
located here. (You'll have the opportunity to visit the real thing
later in your trip at the town of Cordes Junction.) Hour-long
guided tours explaining Soleri's work are offered. Another five

miles further north at 108th and Shea Blvd. is **Taliesin West**, the home of a school of architecture and offices of the Frank Lloyd Wright Foundation. Tours lasting 45 minutes are given by architectural students who explain Wright's methods. Models of famous designs are on display. While this is quite interesting for most people, children will probably be bored beyond belief. Three miles north on Scottsdale Road is **Rawhide**, much more in order for the kids. This is a recreation of an 1880s town. There are rides, more than 20 buildings, a museum with authentic artifacts and shows featuring gunfights and stunts. Allow between one and two hours.

The nearby town of Fountain Hills (located northeast of Scottsdale) has **The Fountain**, a 560-foot-high jet of water that shoots up from a 28-acre lake every hour on the hour and lasts for fifteen minutes. It's like its much more famous cousin in Geneva, Switzerland. A pretty sight, even if it is several miles out of the way.

PHOENIX ODDS AND ENDS: The Phoenix area has more than its share of cultural events. Several theater companies, two operas, a symphony and name entertainment provide year-round diversions to suit every interest. The best place to find out what's going on is in *Where* magazine, distributed free of charge at most hotels.

For those who want to shop 'till they drop, the **Arizona Center** mall is located downtown, and numerous other malls are spread throughout the metro area. There are several Mexican-style markets for those seeking a southwestern flavor. Indian handicrafts are sold in many stores. Scottsdale is especially noted as a shopping mecca. Exclusive shops can be found in the **Borgata**, a shopping village made to resemble an Italian town, in the Fifth Avenue shopping area and **The Scottsdale Galleria**, a beautiful mall that even has a colossal IMAX theater for your entertainment.

Spectator sports are most common in fall and winter when the Suns of the NBA and the Cardinals of the NFL play. Arizona State University teams also have a full schedule of intercollegiate sports. New Years' Day brings the Fiesta Bowl college football game, preceded by an enormous and colorful parade of floats, bands and more. Springtime brings exhibition season for a number of major league baseball teams. There is also horse and dog racing. For those preferring more active sports, Phoenix's extensive park system provides opportunities for every conceivable type of outdoor activity. The dry desert air (especially in winter) is perfect for hot air ballooning. A number of reliable operators can be suggested by the staff at the Visitors' Bureau.

A huge choice of lodging is available. Every chain and even more independent operators are spread throughout the city and surrounding suburbs. Within Phoenix the greatest concentration of hotels and motels is along the I-17 corridor to the north of downtown. Prices, however, are generally lowest in Mesa and Tempe, rising somewhat in Phoenix, and are highest in Scottsdale. The well known resorts are the most expensive places to stay. Although summer rates are *much* lower at the resorts, they can still run you several hundred a night. Some of the more famous places (which are worth a visit even if you won't be staying there) are three **Pointe Hilton Resorts**, the **Arizona Biltmore**, the **Ritz-Carlton**, **Marriott's Camelback Inn**, **The Phoenician**, **The Registry** and the **Scottsdale Princess**. Most of these are located in the Phoenix Mountains/Camelback Mountain area which stretches along the northeast part of Phoenix and into Paradise Valley and Scottsdale.

When you're ready to start exploring nature's splendor, head north out of Phoenix via I-17. It's approximately 60 miles from downtown to Exit 262 and the town of Cordes Junction. From there proceed two miles east (on a dirt road) to **Arcosanti**. This architecturally unique and ecologically friendly prototype community of the future will, when and if ever completed, be home to 5,000 people. Hour-long tours of builder-designer Paolo Soleri's unique vision are given on the hour. Then retrace your route back to the interstate and continue north for 25 miles to Camp Verde (Exit 287). Close by (following signs) is **Montezuma Castle National Monument**. Construction on this cliff dwelling began in the 12th century and it is among the largest and best preserved of any in Arizona or elsewhere. The five-story structure contained 20 rooms. They were accessible only by a ladder that climbed the nearly 50 feet from the base of the cliff to the house. The name was erroneously applied by settlers who thought the structure must have been built by the Aztecs. Visitors are not allowed inside so as to preserve the monument's excellent state of preservation, but the rooms are clearly visible from a trail which leads from the Visitor Center. The Center contains a detailed scale model of the dwelling. Allow 45 minutes for your visit. About 11 miles northeast of the castle via Exit 293 is **Montezuma Well**, a large natural sinkhole measuring almost 500 feet across and over 50 feet deep. Along the rim of the sinkhole are many more cliff dwellings and pueblos. A visit to the Well section of the Monument will require another 75 to 90 minutes, including travel time.

Work your way back to I-17 and this time go south for a brief time, getting off again at Exit 287. Pick up AZ 260 and take it for 13 miles into the town of Cottonwood. From there follow signs leading two miles northwest of town to the **Tuzigoot National Monument**. This huge pueblo is almost a thousand years old and well over a hundred different rooms have been excavated. Thousands of artifacts that were recovered from the site are on display in the Visitor Center. Another 45 minutes is required for visiting this site. Now head back into Cottonwood and, at the junction of US 89A, turn left (northbound). The scenery will quickly change from pleasant to beautiful by the time you traverse the 17 miles to the town of Sedona. This town is at an elevation of 4,000 feet and the heat is far less oppressive than in Phoenix. A small, quiet village not so long ago, Sedona has exploded into a resort and artistic center somewhat like Taos in New Mexico. Accommodations range from the simple to the elegant and prices from moderate to outrageous. Before continuing north from town, take a short detour of three miles on AZ 179 to the **Chapel of the Holy Cross**. This strikingly modern structure sits on top of a ridge and has a commanding view of the surrounding area. It is built of the red rock common to this area and despite its design fits in harmoniously with its surroundings. Go back into Sedona and pick up US 89A once again. You are now about to enter one of Arizona's most beautiful and famous areas – **Oak Creek Canyon**. This spectacular gorge is 16 miles long and generally under a mile wide. Rocky walls towering more than 1,000 feet surround you. The rocks have a distinct reddish color but lighting conditions can change them from copper or bronze to dark brown. The canyon's beauty and eeriness are enhanced by strange monolithic rock formations and buttes both large and small. But Oak Creek is far from a barren place. It is surrounded by surprisingly lush forests and there is plenty of green within the canyon to provide a magnificently colorful display. Late autumn when the trees turn color is a time of exceptional beauty. Along the length of the narrow and winding road (which is easy to drive unless you're pulling a trailer or have a large camper) there are places to pull out. State Parks and waysides have hiking trails into side canyons. The **Oak Creek Vista** near the northern end of the canyon is a place to stop for a truly memorable view. Allow a minimum of an hour for your trip through the canyon alongside the pretty Oak Creek.

Upon emerging from the canyon, you'll pass under I-40 and directly into the town of Flagstaff, largest community in the northern part of the state. By the time you have climbed to Flagstaff (elevation 6,905 feet) you'll be in a part of Arizona that does have four distinct seasons. In fact, there is some excellent skiing available during winter in the vicinity of Flagstaff. Even in summer you can take a chairlift to the **Snow Bowl** at an elevation of 11,500 feet for a splendid view spanning hundreds of miles. Allow about an hour for the chairlift. Actually, the Snow Bowl is 15 miles northwest of town on US 180 and would best be done as a finale to Flagstaff since we'll be proceeding that way later on.

Closer to downtown is the **Museum of Northern Arizona** (located on Fort Valley Road), which is devoted to the natural and cultural history of this portion of the state. Special exhibits deal with the major Indian tribes of northern Arizona. Allow about 30 to 45 minutes. **Riordan State Historic Park** occupies a mansion built by two brothers who were important businessmen at the turn of the century. The large home's exterior is built in a rustic style combining both wood and stone, which leaves you quite unprepared for the very ornate interior that features fine furnishings and even stained-glass windows. Guided tours of the mansion lasting almost an hour are offered throughout the day. The house is surrounded by a small park where you can picnic or relax under some trees. About a mile west of downtown via Santa Fe Avenue is the **Lowell Observatory**. The pure air and clear skies so common to the area are the reasons why the observatory was placed on the top of Mars Hill way back in 1896. An interesting Visitor Center contains the original telescope that was used at the site as well as other exhibits about the work being carried out there. (On some summer evenings visitors can look at the heavens through the huge telescopes; reservations are advised.) Daytime visits should last about one hour.

Approximately 10 miles east of town (use Exit 204 of I-40) is another outstanding group of cliff dwellings. **Walnut Canyon National Monument** encompasses more than 300 dwellings dating from the 12th and 13th centuries, all built within the ledges of a gorge some 400 feet deep. A trail leads past more than two dozen of the dwellings, or you can walk along the canyon rim and get a view of the dwellings from above. There are almost 250 steps along the ruin trail so those with physical limitations should consider skipping that part. You'll be fascinated by the ruins so be sure not to lose sight of the fact that Walnut Canyon, like most of the cliff dwelling sites, is located in a dramatic setting of natural beauty. Allow a minimum of an hour for your visit to Walnut Canyon.

There is a loop leading north out of Flagstaff that covers almost 70 miles before returning to town. It leads to more ruins and other sights. We include it here with the main route because it is so easy to get to, but if you've had your fill of Indian ruins for now (there'll be many more later in the trip), you can skip this part. Consider, too, whether you have the time for it, as the complete loop, including touring time, will take about four to five hours. For those who are going, take US 89 north from town to the town of Antelope Hills (about 25 miles) and turn right into the **Wupatki National Monument**, an area covering almost 36,000 acres. The Monument road leads through about 18 miles and passes by or close to hundreds of separate ruins. The ancestors of the Hopi Indians made this area their home beginning around 1100 A.D. There are numerous self-guiding trails through the ruins, including the one to the 100-room Tall House (the meaning of the word Wupatki). Upon leaving the Monument the road turns south back towards US 89 but before you reach that point you'll pass the **Painted Desert Vista**, where you can look out on a spectacularly colorful area covering hundreds of miles. It feels as if you can see that far when gazing at this giant artist's palette. The road then continues through **Sunset Crater National Monument**. This is the remains of an ancient volcano – a cinder cone rising about 1,000 feet above a huge field of lava flows, spatter cones and other volcanic formations and debris. Rocks in the area range from bright red to black. The name of the Monument comes from the fact that the beautiful shadings of the mountain take on brilliant colors as sunset approaches, but the dazzling array of colors is beautiful at any time of day. Trails lead over lava flows and through a small lava tube. The trails are not that difficult but the uneven and hard rocky surface makes sturdy footwear a necessity.

There are dozens of places to stay in Flagstaff. Chains include **Best Western, Choice (Comfort, EconoLodge and Quality), Days Inn, Holiday Inn, Super 8, TraveLodge** and others. A wide selection of restaurants is also here, but those looking for a quick and inexpensive meal should try **Furr's Cafeteria** at Exit 195B of I-40.

We'll leave Flagstaff and head northwest via US 180 through the San Francisco Mountains of the Coconino National Forest. Arizona's highest mountains are located in this area, but the scenic route climbs easily over them before dropping down about 5,000 feet to the top of the Coconino Plateau. It is about 50 miles from Flagstaff to the town of Bedrock City. Then you'll travel for just under 30 miles more before reaching, yes, the Grand Canyon! The flat plateau is a wonderful way to get to the canyon because you are totally unprepared for the vista that awaits you. Not that anyone could adequately prepare for the sights to be found at **Grand Canyon National Park**, an awesome place that is justifiably one of the world's most famous sights. Our visit for now will be limited to the more popular South Rim (the more remote North Rim is included in one of the Alternative Routes). Its statistics are so staggering that they require some enumeration before we start touring. The Canyon is 277 miles long. Its width varies from a minimum of four miles to a maximum of 21. The South Rim is an average of 4,500 feet above the canyon floor (the north is over a mile high). The mile-wide Colorado River at the bottom of the canyon barely looks like a silver thread from this height. Then there are the colors – while you'll see almost every imaginable shade, the purple hues are the most common and most dramatic. The history of the earth is revealed in its countless layers.

Seeing the Grand Canyon is almost too easy. An excellent road traverses the entire South Rim providing access to the many over-looks by means of very short trails. The South Rim roads are divided into an East Rim Drive and a West Rim Drive. The purpose of mentioning this is that the West Rim Drive is closed to private vehicles during the summer – you have to take the free open air tram shuttle, which is actually a more relaxing and enjoyable way to travel. You can also take a short or miles-long walk on the trail that parallels the road alongside the entire South Rim of the can-yon. Every view of the canyon is different. The major viewpoints along the West Rim Drive are Trailview Overlook, Maricopa Point, Hopi Point, Mojave Point, The Abyss, Pima Point and Hermit's Rest at the end. At the Powell Memorial Overlook there is a monu-ment to the famous explorer John Wesley Powell. The 26-mile East Rim Drive is somewhat less crowded but also contains outstanding view points – including Yavapai, Mather, Grandview, Moran and Lipan Points. Yavapai Point also has a museum devoted to local Indians. The Tusayan Indian ruin and museum provides a brief change of pace coming just before Lipan Point. The easternmost viewpoint is Desert View where you'll look out on the Painted Desert as well as the canyon from the Watchtower, a tall, round structure built in the 1930s to resemble the architectural style of the cliff dwelling Indians.

It will take a minimum of a half-day and most likely longer just to ride along the South Rim roads, take in most if not all of the viewpoints, experience for at least a while a walk along the rim and visit the several interesting museums and Visitor Centers. Then we come to the question of going down into the canyon. Trekking into the canyon is extremely popular, as it should be, for new adventures and vistas await those who make the journey. But it is a difficult trip in both directions and not for the faint of heart (either physically or emotionally). Unless you are an experienced climber, you should restrict yourself to ranger-conducted hikes. The famous mule trips are another option but they too require a degree of stamina above being able to cope with a sore rear end. There are also weight restrictions. Mule trips last from several hours to three days. Those hiking into the canyon need a minimum of a day – more if you are going to be doing the entire Bright Angel Trail across the canyon and up to the North Rim. Many people will want to get "into" the Grand Canyon. Consult the National Park Service for information before taking any trip into the canyon.

You'll almost certainly be staying overnight in the Park and there are six lodges along the South Rim, mostly in the vicinity of Grand Canyon Village. Prices are high but the accommodations are better than you will find in many National Parks. Reservations should be made well in advance. There are also several places to stay within a few miles south of the park entrance, including some of the well-known chains. Dining at the Grand Canyon is no problem as the hotels have full service restaurants and cafeterias to fit your style and budget.

Evening activities at the canyon include many talks and ranger-conducted campfire programs. You can also take in a beautiful IMAX film about the canyon. The theater is nine miles south of Grand Canyon Village, outside the park. It is not affiliated with the Park Service.

Exit from the eastern end (AZ 64) of the park, a distance of 31 miles from Desert View to the town of Cameron. (This may mean having to drive the East Rim again if you had gone back to Canyon Village to spend the night.) The entire route is one of marvelous scenery, but especially the segment that passes through the **Little Colorado River Gorge**. This narrow and deep gorge will at least put the Grand Canyon out of your mind for the moment. There are several outstanding view points where you can stop.

At the town of Cameron go north (left turn) on US 89. It is an 82-mile drive from there to the town of Page, located a few miles from the Utah state line. Most of the ride passes through nice scenery, including portions of the Painted Desert and atop the Kaibito Plateau. Page is a large town that came into existence to house the workers who built the Glen Canyon Dam. It is the gateway to our next series of attractions, highlighted by the vast **Glen Canyon National Recreation Area**. Page is a good place to make your base as there is a good choice of motels within the town, and more luxurious resorts within a few miles along the lake shore's southwestern corner.

Your visit to the recreation area should begin at the **Glen Canyon Dam** and its adjoining Carl Harden Visitor Center. The center has excellent exhibits, explaining the huge dam's construction process and operations, along with large relief maps of the area around the dam. There is an observation deck outside with a great view of not only the dam but the deep, dark and forbidding canyon which it crosses. The walls are a dark red and the relative narrowness of the canyon doesn't allow much sunlight to hit bottom. As a result the river's water appears almost black. The dam itself can be explored by either a self-guiding or ranger-conducted tour that takes you to the base. From there you'll see the giant turbines and also get a completely different perspective as you look up at the gracefully curving arc of the dam, the canyon and the highway bridge which crosses it. Allow about an hour to tour the dam and Visitor Center.

A few miles to the north at the Wahweap Marina is the departure point for five-hour and full-day boat tours on **Lake Powell**. This is the best way to see Glen Canyon unless you are adept at hiking in difficult back-country canyon terrain. The vast recreation area connects Grand Canyon National Park with **Canyonlands National Park** in Utah. The area was once a canyon-filled desert but Lake Powell changed all that. Now the beautiful blue waters of the lake are surrounded by red sandstone cliffs. Sometimes they soar to great heights as at Navajo Mountain, but often taking the form of low, unusually shaped hills. One looks like a dragon and was so named by the locals. The boat ride is a pleasant way to see the sights (assuming you haven't brought along your own vessel, which can be put into the water at one of several marinas). But people with a lot of time can rent a houseboat and float on Lake Powell for days, fishing and soaking up the sun and sights. The all-day tour goes further down the lake and explores more side canyons, but both trips provide great scenery and a stop at the breathtaking **Rainbow Bridge National Monument**. This, like a good part of the lake, is in Utah. The natural bridge is not visible until you are very close to it because it is hidden in a side canyon with high walls. It is one of nature's great spectacles – 290 feet high and about 275 feet across. Time is allowed for you to walk right up to the bridge, to walk underneath it and get a dizzying view that cannot be described.

Upon returning to the marina you should go back into Page and stop for a half-hour or so at the **John Wesley Powell Museum**, which documents the local Indian cultures and geology of the Colorado River but mainly commemorates the many explorations of Mr. Powell who, among other things, gave the Grand Canyon its name.

From the time you leave Page until you reach I-40 pay particular attention to the locations mentioned for lodging. These are just about the only decent accommodations or good food, and even gas can sometimes be difficult to find. Take AZ 98 from Page for 66 miles through the high desert until it reaches US 160. Follow the latter route eastbound and you'll pass through the **Navajo National Monument**. Although this area contains many fine examples of cliff dwellings in often spectacular settings, they are all very difficult to reach, the easiest still requiring a strenuous five-mile round trip. Therefore, most readers will probably skip it except, perhaps, for a brief stop at the Visitor Center. Further along on US 160 is the cutoff for the town of Kayenta. Food, lodging and gas are available here (would you believe a **Holiday Inn** in this remote place?). It is also the way to Monument Valley, which is described in the Utah chapter and can be made a side trip to your Arizona journey (see the Alternative Routes section). Stay on US 160 for eight miles past the junction for Kayenta and then take Indian Reservation Route 59. This traverses 57 miles of the Black Mesa through the Navajo Indian Reservation. The road isn't great but it's paved and shouldn't present any unusual difficulty. It ends at US 191 where you'll turn right and head south 14 miles more to the town of Chinle (food, gas and lodging available).

Two miles east of town is the rugged and spectacular country of **Canyon de Chelly National Monument** (pronounced *d'shea* as in the name of the baseball stadium). This site was occupied by ancient Indian cultures as far back as 350 A.D. and was continuously occupied for about a thousand years. Today the more than 85,000 acres of the monument provide a living archaeological preserve with some of the most beautiful scenery to be found anywhere. Canyon de Chelly is 26 miles long and is adjoined by another formerly occupied canyon that stretches for 35 more miles. The reddish sandstone cliffs are a mere 30 feet high in the vicinity of the informative Visitor Center, but rapidly rise to over 1,000 feet at the end of the canyon. The drops are sheer and the cliffs unusually smooth. No, Virginia, people did not sand them down – it's more of nature's incredible handiwork. The many ruins at the top of the cliffs on either side of the canyon give the overall impression of a fortress and so it must have seemed to anyone who would have wanted to attack the large community. After taking in the exhibits at the Visitor Center you can drive along either the North or South Rim. Both routes are almost identical in length (about 21 miles) and pass fine examples of ruins, with many view points where the canyon can be seen in all of its glory. The South Rim road passes places with names such as Wild Cherry (a canyon) and formations called Face Rock and Spider Rock. It is also the way to get to the **White House Overlook and Trail**, the only trail in the monument that can be explored on your own. The monument is administered by the Park Service but is owned by the Navajo and people do live here. Don't wander off on your own as the prohibitions are strictly enforced. The trail leads to the impressive **White House Ruin**. The North Rim road will take you to **Ledge Ruin, Antelope House, Mummy Cave** (archaeologists found well-preserved bodies in the cave) and **Massacre Cave** among the many dramatic views along the road. There is a gain in elevation along the roads from 5,500 feet to a maximum of about 7,000. Each rim road requires a round-trip of about two hours including view stops. The White House Trail is fairly difficult and takes at least an additional hour. If you want to take other trails inquire at the Visitor Center about obtaining the services of a Park Ranger or authorized Navajo guide. Four-wheel and jeep tours into the canyon itself can be arranged in the town of Chinle and the rugged country provides some awesome sights.

Once you get back to Chinle continue south on US 191. It is 75 miles from this point to the junction of I-40. Almost exactly half-way there is the town of Ganado and a mile west on AZ 264 is the **Hubbell Trading Post National Historic Site**. The Hubbell family established the post to trade with the Navajo back in the late 1870s and for many years the trading post was the only means of obtaining goods from the outside world for the Navajo tribe. The post has passed from Hubbell family control but it is still active. This makes it an especially interesting place to visit because in addition to the historical exhibits you have the opportunity to experience what goes on in a real Indian trading post. Hopefully you have been able to restrain yourself from buying too many Indian craft souvenirs (especially bogus ones) because Hubbell's is possibly the best place in Arizona to choose from a wide selection of handicrafts at reasonable prices. The historic site doesn't take that long to visit but do allow some time to browse through the crafts.

The town of Chambers is the site of a **Best Western** hotel and takes you off the Indian reservations you have been on (with the exception of Page and the Glen Canyon National Recreation Area) since leaving the Grand Canyon. Take I-40 westbound for 22 miles to Exit 311. Almost immediately upon leaving the highway you'll come to the Visitor Center of the **Petrified Forest National Park**, another of Arizona's premier attractions.

This large area was a thick forest about 200 million years ago and time has made an enormous transformation of the land. Remains of trees large and small, some standing, but mostly lying on their side and broken into fragments, are scattered throughout the park in an amazing variety of colors and looking every bit like jewels or glass. The northern section of the park encompasses a particularly stunning section of the **Painted Desert**.

A good road traverses the narrow park from north to south, a distance of 27 miles. Virtually all of the major sites are accessible from the road. Upon leaving the Visitor Center the road twists and turns dramatically, revealing a splendid panorama – the Painted Desert. Numerous overlooks within a very short distance of one another provide plenty of opportunity for you to stop the car, get out and drink from nature's cup. As the transition to the petrified log area begins you also encounter formations known as **The Tepees**, the name being obvious upon sight of these inverted V-shaped hills with brightly colored layer upon layer. Now you will see the petrified logs in great numbers. Nowhere are they more beautiful than off of a short spur road leading to an area called the Blue Mesa. Visible from the main road is **Agate Bridge**, the longest (100 feet) unbroken petrified tree in the park, although it is now supported to prevent it from splitting in two. Overlooks with names like Jasper Forest, Crystal Forest, Rainbow Forest and Long Logs give you an idea of the array of sights that you'll see. Mostly everything is within a short walk of the road, although there is a lengthy trail in the Long Logs section. In addition to the Visitor Center, there is the small **Rainbow Forest Museum** near the southern end of the Park. Allow about three hours for your visit to

Petrified Forest, or more if you intend to go hiking any great distance. Be prepared for the heat and carry water. Much of the petrified wood is small and can be easily picked up, but it is illegal to remove any of it from the park.

Upon leaving the Petrified Forest you will be on US 180. Take it west for 18 miles into the town of Holbrook. A dozen or so motels are available here, including a few **Best Westerns**, a **Days Inn** and a **Comfort Inn**. From Holbrook you'll drive south on AZ 77 for 47 miles to the town of Show Low. By this time the northern Arizona desert is behind you and the terrain becomes dominated by national forests and the mountains of the Mogollon Rim. Near town are the attractive **Fool Hollow Lake** and an easy 1 1/2-mile trail leading to the **Mogollon Rim Overlook**. The latter can be reached by going seven miles south of Show Low on AZ 260. The town also has a couple of decent motels.

We'll take US 60 west from Show Low (although the prevailing direction here is actually south) for 81 miles to Globe. This stretch of highway is very scenic with numerous roadside pullouts and rest areas that make it easier to take in what nature has to offer. Among the sights you'll see are the **Salt River Canyon**, a five-mile-wide gorge with vertical drops of 1,500-2,000 feet and topped by unusual rock formations. Globe began as a mining town in the 1880s. You can stop here overnight as there are a few good motels. It is a fine base for rafting tours on the Salt River. The route between Globe and Phoenix (known as the Apache Trail) is one of the more scenic ones in the state but is not on our main itinerary – see the Alternative Routes for details. You'll continue south on AZ 77 from Globe all the way to Tucson, a distance of exactly 100 miles. The route is pretty but undistinguished by Arizona standards.

About two-thirds of the way to Tucson, just south of the town of Oracle, is the **Biosphere 2**. This unusual attraction is actually a working laboratory in which several tropical ecosystems are contained within an airtight structure. It was built to see how an ecosystem could recycle the necessary ingredients for sustaining life. You may remember having read in the newspapers or seen on TV that the experimental methods used at Biosphere came under a lot of criticism from some members of the scientific community. Regardless, the almost two-hour tour of Biosphere 2 is of unusual interest.

AZ 77 will bring you into the heart of downtown Tucson where the first priority should be to ditch your car since heavy traffic will be an impediment to touring. There are many garages or you can feed the meters near the University of Arizona.

Tucson has grown from a small town to a city of a half-million people, second largest in the state. Like Phoenix it is in a high desert valley surrounded by mountains. However, the elevation is higher than Phoenix so the climate is not as hot, though summer days in the high 90s are the rule. It's apparent that many people like the combination of warm, dry weather and cloudless skies because that has certainly been a factor in Tucson's growth. Cloudy days are a rarity.

While almost every major American city, including Tucson, has become a mix of ethnic backgrounds and different cultures, perhaps no city has such a pervasive Mexican cultural influence as Tucson. Mexicans comprise the largest single group and you would be hard pressed to find more of a Mexican influence anywhere without actually crossing the border.

Seeing Tucson can be a bit difficult. There is a grid pattern throughout much of the city, although it seems to get lost in parts of downtown. And even though there are many attractions throughout the metropolitan area, they tend to be more scattered than in most of the larger cities we've visited. We'll divide things up by whether the attraction is downtown, west, north or east of downtown. Some attractions in nearby suburbs will be described later since our continuing journey will bring us in a loop southeast of Tucson and back again.

A good place to begin our tour is on the campus of the **University of Arizona** where there are several interesting attractions. Start at the intersection of Park Avenue and 6th Street, which forms the southwestern corner of the University and the northeastern corner of downtown. You can walk around the attractive campus, but four blocks north is the **Arizona State Museum**, home of one of the best Southwestern archaeological collections of any museum in the world. The extensive exhibits describe both the human and natural history of the region. Allow about 45 minutes. Several blocks west on University Blvd. is the **Flandrau Science Center**. The center covers a wide range of physical sciences including astronomy and the space sciences. Many of the exhibits are geared toward visitor participation and are fun for both children and adults. If you visit in the evening the 16-inch telescope in the observatory can be used at no additional charge. The Center's Dome Theater has an excellent planetarium show. These performances last an hour and the main part of the Center will take roughly another hour to see properly.

Other places on campus that you may find of interest include the **University of Arizona Museum of Art** (major works of art from Medieval times forward, 30 minutes), the **Center for Creative Photography** (more than 50,000 photographs and display of techniques for taking better pictures, 30 minutes minimum) and several smaller museums on such diverse topics as mineralogy and pharmacy.

Now go back a few blocks to 6th Street and turn right. Proceed to N. Main and make a left turn, continuing until you reach the **Tucson Museum of Art**. Don't say "Oh, no, we just saw an art museum." This one is different because it is devoted solely to art of the western hemisphere, with particular emphasis on the Pre-Columbian period and the works of Western American artists. The complex also includes two of Tucson's oldest buildings, the **Edward Nye Fish House** and **La Casa Cordova**, the latter being from 1850. It houses a Mexican heritage collection. Allow about an hour to tour the main museum and its associated structures.

After seeing La Casa Cordova your appetite to explore the older, original Spanish and Mexican section of Tucson should have been whetted. That's good because this is a good place to embark on such a walking tour. The surrounding blocks, especially those just north of the Museum are filled with many examples of architecture from the late 1840s through near the end of the 19th century.

Immediately south of this area in the Community Center on Granada Avenue is the **John C. Fremont House** which served as the residence of the Territorial Governor. The structure was built in the 1860s and is furnished in period.

This completes the "downtown" tour, so it's time to get back in the car once again, although the first ride is a short one. From wherever you parked head north until you reach Broadway. Turn west and proceed across the Santa Cruz River (just after I-10) and turn left on Cuesta following signs for Sentinel Peak Road into **Sentinel Peak Park**, sometimes referred to as "A Mountain" because of the huge letter "A" that is emblazoned on the side of the mountain. The letter represents the University of Arizona and it has become a standard annual ritual for the freshmen class to whitewash it. However, the reason for going here is not to see the big letter, but to see the big view of Tucson and its mountains.

Speedway Boulevard is a major east-to-west thoroughfare in the northern part of the town and will be used to get to a number of outstanding attractions west of the downtown area. The first of these is the **International Wildlife Museum**. There are displays of more than 300 different mounted animals placed in life-like dioramas. The art of taxidermy is explained and there are exhibits and film presentations on wildlife, game parks of the world, and endangered species. The building in which the Museum is housed is also of interest because it is patterned after a Saharan fort of the French Foreign Legion – we're not sure why, but it does make a nice picture! Allow a minimum of 45 minutes, and more if you plan to view some of the films offered.

Speedway Blvd. becomes the Gates Pass Road and leads directly into the 17,000-acre **Tucson Mountain Park**. One of Tucson's most popular attractions is in the park itself and that is **Old Tucson Studios**. The "town" was constructed in 1939 for the filming of the motion picture *Arizona*, but the movie industry knew they had a good thing going so they continued using the site and have filmed literally hundreds of movies, TV shows and commercials here. Today thousands of visitors have fun exploring a "dangerous" mine, riding on a stagecoach, looking at how stuntmen and women perform their trade and witnessing gunfights. It should take about 90 minutes to see all of this, that is, if your kids can drag you away.

Tucson Mountain Park, aside from its many recreational opportunities such as trails and horseback riding, also contains a large variety of desert vegetation. The Sonoran desert of southern Arizona is far different from the northern Arizona deserts and is probably more what you think a desert "should" look like. Among the species here are the stately saguaro cactus. Even more of these can be seen immediately to the north of Tucson Mountain Park in the West or Tucson Mountain Unit of the **Saguaro National Monument**. There is an information center here as well as a six-mile loop road that will take you through dense stands of saguaro. Besides the loop road you can make closer contact with the desert vegetation along two short trails called the Cactus Garden Trail and the Desert Discovery Nature Trail. Allow about an hour for your visit to the West unit of the Monument. More about the other unit a little later.

After completing the Monument head back into Tucson Mountain Park and stop at the famous **Arizona-Sonora Desert Museum**, the foremost such facility on the Sonoran environment to be found anywhere. Besides displaying both wildlife and vegetation unique to this region, the Museum depicts the natural history of the Sonora with a walk-through model of a limestone cave and exhibits on the forces that have built it such as volcanos and other forms of seismic action. This is a unique and educational attraction worth exploring for a minimum of 90 minutes.

Now it's time to see other parts of the city. Exit from Tucson Mountain Park from the south (Kinney Road), which will run into Ajo Way. Turn left and stay on Ajo until I-10, heading east on that road to Exit 268 (Valencia Road). That street will take you to the **Pima Air and Space Museum**. Adjacent to Davis-Monthan Air Force Base, the museum has an excellent collection of almost 200 aircraft from the earliest days of flight right up through the jet age. Both military and commercial aircraft are on display including many famous models. Allow 45 minutes to an hour for touring the collection.

After the Air Museum, continue east on Valencia for about two miles to Kolb Road. Then head north to just north of the intersection with Speedway Blvd., turning right onto Tanque Verde Road (cross over the bridge). Follow signs (left turn) into Sabino Canyon Road and drive on it for approximately three more miles to the **Visitor Center of Sabino Canyon**. The Center houses exhibits about this beautiful natural area and is also the place where you can board a free shuttle that will transport you four miles through the canyon (no private vehicles allowed). A lovely creek winds through the narrow desert canyon. You can walk to your heart's content within the main canyon, although the more active may be interested in exploring some of the much longer and more difficult trails that are within some of the side canyons. Information is available at the Visitor Center. Assuming that you restrict yourself to the main canyon, your visit should take about 45 minutes. Then reverse your route, taking Kolb Blvd. back into the heart of the city. The main itinerary continues in an easterly direction.

TUCSON ODDS AND ENDS: Tucson offers a full schedule of theater events, though not on the same level as Phoenix. Much activity is centered at the University of Arizona. The same is true for spectator sports, except that the Tucson area is very active during the exhibition baseball season. Soccer is quite popular in the area, and there are two leagues that play throughout the year. Tucson's parks are many and diverse, offering outdoor activities of every kind year-round.

The area also has many malls but more authentic southwestern and Mexican crafts are better found in the shops of the Old Town area or in the downtown shopping district on 4th Avenue between 4th and 7th Streets.

There aren't that many hotels downtown, but a Holiday Inn, La Quinta and Ramada are among them and prices are generally under $100 per night. Otherwise, lodging is spread out, with major concentrations near the airport and along Speedway Blvd. near where it intersects I-10. Prices aren't that different from downtown although there are some real bargains here and there. The only super-expensive places are some of the resorts in the foothills of the Catalina Mountains to the north of the city.

Restaurants will accommodate every taste but while you are in Tucson you should sample the authentic Mexican cuisine. Your hotel staff can usually provide the name and location of a restaurant close to where you're staying since there are many such establishments throughout the city.

Let's continue now with the main itinerary. Head east on Broadway, which eventually becomes the Old Spanish Trail. In about 15 miles you'll reach the **East** or **Rincon Mountain Unit of Saguaro National Monument**. Sounds familiar, but it is different enough from the West Unit to make the time visiting it worthwhile. In fact, visitors will probably be evenly divided as to which part of the Monument they like better. The Rincon Mountain area contains an eight-mile loop road (this one is fully paved) that will take you past some of the largest specimens of saguaro cactus to be found anywhere. Many are as high as 30 or 40 feet and you might even catch a glimpse of some that tower more than 50 feet. While their density is less here than in the West Unit, the taller trees are concentrated primarily in this section. There is also an informative Visitor Center and some trails in this larger section of the Monument. Allow about an hour.

Upon leaving the Monument continue along the Old Spanish Trail and in a few miles you'll come to the **R. W. Webb Winery**. Although many visitors are surprised to learn that Arizona produces any wine, the fact is that this part of the state has several wineries. This one is the largest and they offer 30-minute tours of the wine production process followed by free tastings.

A few more miles down the same road is **Colossal Cave**. This is a limestone cave like many others found throughout the United States. However, most caves are "wet" caves, that is, water seepage is continuing the process of building new formations. Colossal Cave is dry – there are many beautiful formations to be seen but they are no longer growing. Tours lasting 45 minutes cover a little under one mile out of the more than six miles of known passageways. There are a lot of steps but it isn't overly difficult and the cave has a very comfortable temperature year round.

From the cave it is five more miles until you reach I-10. Head east to the town of Benson (Exit 303, Best Western motel located in town) and pick up AZ 80 for 23 miles south to the town of Tombstone. The entire town has been designated the **Tombstone National Historic Site**, a most unusual status for a community in the United States. The 1870s brought prosperity in the form of gold and silver mining. It also brought with it lawlessness that has become famous in the annals of American history and folklore. The shootout at the OK Corral between Wyatt Earp and the Clanton gang has taken on legendary proportions. A visit to Tombstone is both fun and informative.

When you arrive in town on AZ 80 the first attraction you come to is **Boothill Graveyard**, where the local citizenry lie side by side with almost 200 villains. The town can best be explored entirely on foot since virtually all of the other attractions are located within a small area bounded by adjacent Freemont and Allen Streets running between 3rd and 6th Streets. Everything looks pretty much as it did during the late 19th century. Highlights include the **Historama**, where animated figures tell you all about Tombstone – "the town too tough to die." Presentations begin on the hour and then you can proceed directly into the **O.K. Corral**, site of the great gun battle. If you happen to be here at 2 PM on the first and third Sunday of the month, the spectacle of the Earp-Clanton fight is recreated. The **Bird Cage Saloon** was the largest and most opulent of the town's many wild establishments. This one had a theater and dance hall in addition to the bar. The interior has remained exactly as it was in the 1880s. Among other buildings that you'll want to visit or at least pass by are the newspaper offices of the Tombstone Epitaph Building, the Rose Tree Inn Museum, containing a rose bush planted in 1885 and now encompassing about 8,000 square feet (and still growing), The Silver Nugget Museum, and the Crystal Palace Saloon. One part of town that isn't contained in the National Historic Site but is state-owned is the **Tombstone Courthouse State Historic Park**. This building served as the county courthouse until the county seat was relocated to another town in the late 1920s. It now documents the history of Tombstone and the surrounding area.

Most of the places in town take less than a half-hour to visit on an individual basis but, due to the number of attractions and the fun you can have just strolling through the streets, you should allocate about three hours for a complete visit. Lodging is limited in town but there are a few places to stay (including another Best Western) and restaurants are plentiful. You can still get a drink at many of the saloons (even if it is a soft drink in some cases).

Tombstone is near some very scenic areas, and you'll be driving through them as you leave town via AZ 92 to the south and pass through the **San Pedro Riparian National Conservation Area**. It's about 20 miles from Tombstone to the town of Sierra Vista, a fast developing community next to a sprawling army base. The **Mile High Ramsey Canyon Preserve** is a beautiful area of surprisingly lush vegetation in a deep canyon. The area contains many hiking and nature trails which you can explore, but most of them are on the difficult side.

From town you can get to the main gate of Fort Huachuca, get a pass and proceed for two miles to the **Fort Huachuca Museum**. The fort was built to protect white settlers from the Apache Indians. While those days may long since be gone, it has remained an active military installation through two world wars and is now involved in high tech communications for the army. The museum traces the role of the fort, especially during the pioneer days, and contains many fine displays and exhibits. Allow a minimum of a half-hour. Outside you'll see rows of buildings built as administrative centers and barracks during the 19th century still being used today for the same purpose. Despite the presence of many modern buildings, you can, with a little imagination, place yourself back in the days when the cavalry was really the cavalry.

Inquire at the Fort whether you can exit through the north gate. If so, it is four miles to AZ 82, where you'll turn left/west. On the other hand, if the army decides to be fussy and send you back through the main gate, it will be necessary for you to go back to Tombstone and pick up AZ 82 at that point. AZ 82 crosses high desert, national forests and rolling hills that are home to Arizona's cattle and horse industries. On the way is the town of **Patagonia**. An interesting stop in town is the **Museum of the Horse**, with a nice collection of horse-drawn carriages and riding accessories such as saddles.

It is under 20 miles from Patagonia to the city of **Nogales** on the U.S.-Mexican border. While there isn't much of interest on the American side (although there are several places to stay overnight), most people who come to town cross into Mexico for some heavy shopping. If this is for you, we suggest that you leave your car on the American side and cross the border by foot, which is much quicker and easier than driving. No passport is required but you do need some proof of citizenship in order to return to the States or for an instant tourist permit at the border. (This is good for up to 72 hours in Mexico but is only required if you are going to be traveling beyond the border towns). The stores and shops begin as soon as you get over the border and the mostly English-speaking merchants are only too eager to do business with you. Don't be afraid to bargain. Payment in U.S. currency or by credit card is just as good as pesos (maybe better). Each adult is allowed to bring back up to $400 worth of goods without paying any customs duties. While this kind of activity doesn't appeal to everyone on vacation, it can be a lot of fun if you've never been to Mexico (although you certainly can't judge Mexico by a few blocks of shopping on the U.S. border).

Interstate 19 connects Nogales with Tucson, a distance of 65 miles, but we have a few things to see before getting back. Immediately adjacent to Exit 29 is the **Tumacacori National Historic Park**. Construction of a large mission and protecting fort began around the year 1800 but was abandoned in the late 1840s due to a combination of constant Apache raids and opposition from the Mexican government. Today, the historic park comprises the ruins of the Tumacacori Mission and two smaller nearby missions. Enough ruins remain to show the distinct southwestern mission architecture. A modern museum built in the Sonoran architectural style documents the history of the mission and surrounding area. Allow 45 minutes to visit the site. Nearby at Exit 34 is the **Tubac Presidio**

State Historic Park. This older mission was begun in the 1750s by the Spaniards. A fort was built around the mission to protect the occupants from Indian attack. The site today contains remains of a fort from the 1850s; you can go underground to view the original walls and foundations. There is also a good museum in the park, for which another 30-45 minutes should be allocated. The town of Tubac is an attractive place alongside a river and is popular as an artists' colony. Several galleries in town display works for sale.

Leave the Interstate again, this time at Exit 69, and travel west for less than a mile to the **Titan Missile Museum**, sure to be one of the most unusual places you've ever visited. At one time there were over 50 Titan missile sites in the United States. All have been dismantled except for this one which has been converted into a museum. Museum, however, is not quite the right word – for this is the real thing. Hour-long tours will conduct you through an actual underground silo where a real Titan missile still stands, seemingly ready for launch (but it isn't armed). Perhaps even more interesting, though less dramatic, is the portion of the tour that takes you into the launch control operations room, 100 feet beneath the surface. You have to climb down steps to get to it so the physically impaired should think twice before coming to the Museum. Tour guides explain all about the operations of the base during its active years from the early 1960s through 1982.

Once you've completed the Titan site, get back on I-19 and take it to Exit 92. Proceed west once again for about a mile to the magnificent **Mission San Xavier del Bac**, located on an Indian reservation. The present building dates from 1783, having taken almost 16 years to complete. It is considered by many to be one of the most beautiful Spanish-style missions in America and has earned the name the "White Dove of the Desert." It is still a functioning church, a missionary church at that, and it still tends to the spiritual and physical needs of the Tohono O'odham Indians living on the reservation. The builders didn't have a lot of money so the interior is made with simple materials. This is not to say that it looks simple for it has been painstakingly painted to resemble marble, tile and other materials richer than those available. There is also an outdoor replica of the Grotto of Lourdes. Allow about an hour for your visit.

In a few minutes I-19 will bring you back into Tucson where you can continue your sightseeing if you wish; or link up with I-10 and head north back towards Phoenix. Arizona's two largest cities are about two hours apart (115 miles) by superhighway, but our route is a little longer because of an important detour.

The final stop along the way is another Indian ruin site, but a most impressive and interesting one – in case you or your children are starting to get ruinitis. Use Exit 211 from I-10 and proceed north on AZ 87 for 19 miles to the **Casa Grande Ruins National Monument**. The site dates back almost 700 years and was occupied until sometime in the 1400s. The centerpiece of the Monument is one of the largest Pre-Columbian Indian dwellings in the country – a four-story structure made of mud. The walls are almost five feet thick at the base and narrow at the top. Archaeologists have yet to figure out for sure the purpose of the building's 11 rooms, but it may have served as an astronomical observatory or some type of ceremonial center – perhaps both. Around the structure are numerous other ruins of the village, all of which were surrounded by a wall. The Visitor Center shows what the village looked like when occupied and examines the possible reasons why this tribe and so many others like them vanished within a relatively short period. Allow at least an hour for visiting Casa Grande, which covers a large area.

After leaving the ruins, continue on AZ 87 for four more miles to the junction with AZ 387. This road will bring you back to the Interstate in 10 miles. After 35 more miles you will be back into Phoenix where, if you are concluding your trip and heading back to the airport, you can take I-10 to Exit 149 for Sky Harbor. Those going on can branch off of I-10 onto I-17 and use Exit 195B for entry into downtown Phoenix.

Alternative Routes

So you still want to do more. Or maybe you want to do less. That's okay because here we introduce our final series of experiments in trip behavior modification. This section will offer seven different options, four of which are simple side-trip extensions from the main route. Two are ways of cutting off a portion of the trip for those who have less time; they do so by covering a splendidly scenic part of the state with lots to see and do (which is where we'll begin). The final alternative route is a potentially long haul that we won't even attempt to describe here.

THE APACHE TRAIL (GLOBE TO PHOENIX) CUTOFF: This alternative can be used to cut the main itinerary into two distinct sections, namely northern and southern Arizona. It connects the town of Globe with Phoenix by one of two methods, the longer one being 100 miles of more difficult roads and the shorter method covering about 90 on an easier route (but with less scenery). Although it's possible to add this to the main route in a number of ways, it would make for quite a lengthy trip.

Both methods head east from Globe on US 60 but diverge a few miles later at the junction of AZ 88. We'll cover the longer route first, which is via AZ 88, better known as the Apache Trail. This spectacular route was built along the path of an ancient Apache Indian route in 1905 to facilitate the construction of the Roosevelt Dam. It is primitive country all along the 78-mile route, 25 of which are narrow, winding and unpaved. Actually, the whole route is narrow and winding but the gravel portion and driving at the edge of precipitous cliffs will deter some travelers. The road is well maintained and only presents a hazard during rainy weather, which isn't all that likely. The Superstition Mountains are steeped in legend, especially that of the Lost Dutchman Goldmine. Whether it actually existed is a matter of conjecture but it is fact that people have lost their lives looking for it. There are many long and often difficult trails along the entire route, but plenty of opportunity for easy sightseeing as well. Tours on horseback are popular and can be arranged in Apache Junction at the end of the route.

Now for the sights you'll see. **Roosevelt Lake** is impounded by the dam of the same name and is 23 miles long and up to two miles wide. It is where the gravel portion of the road begins. **Apache Lake** is 17 miles long and was created by the Horse Mesa Dam. From the Apache Lake Vista you can peer down into the canyon that envelopes the lake – it's quite a sight. **Fish Creek Canyon** is one of the most spectacular portions of the entire trail. Walls reaching almost 2,000 feet above the canyon floor (and road) surround you in a dazzling, colorful array. Then comes 10-mile-long **Canyon Lake** in a wild and dramatic gorge that is visible from another overlook. This is where the best (or worst) part of the road begins, depending upon your outlook. It falls 500 feet in three miles through a series of hair-raising drops and turns. Where the road reaches lake level there is a marina and you can take a 90-minute boat tour through the beautiful scenery (and give the car driver a chance to recapture his or her senses). The **Needles Vista Viewpoint** allows you to get a clear look at this soaring pinnacle that rises from the Superstition Mountains. The final attraction as you near Apache Junction is the **Goldfield Ghost Town and Mine Tour**. Besides exploring the mine you can walk through this recreation of a western town complete with entertainment and gunfights. As it is near to town it is something you can do even if you are taking the other route from Globe. Not counting time for the boat ride or Goldfield (which requires about an hour), you should figure that a half-day will be spent traversing the Apache Trail.

Those who have been scared off can continue on US 60 all the way from Globe to Apache Junction, a distance of 45 miles. The road, especially the first half out of Globe, is very scenic as it crosses the rugged Pinal Mountains. You'll get plenty of good views and pass through a long tunnel. One of the best sights along this route is the forbidding Devil's Canyon. A major stop nearby is at the **Boyce Thompson Southwestern Arboretum** in the town of Superior. This establishment covers more than 400 acres and contains over 1,500 different varieties of plants. Hundreds of birds and other forms of wildlife roam through the arboretum as well. There are short and easy trails and an interesting Visitor Center. Allow between 60 and 90 minutes to tour the Arboretum.

FLAGSTAFF TO HOLBROOK CUTOFF: This option covers about 125 miles and will result in saving over 300 miles from the suggested itinerary, eliminating everything between the Grand Canyon and Petrified Forest National Parks. That misses some great scenery, including the Canyon de Chelly, so use this option only if you need to lop a couple of days from the time needed to do the main route.

Head for the Grand Canyon immediately after passing through Oak Creek Canyon and return to Flagstaff via the Little Colorado River Gorge, Wupatki National Monument, and the other attractions along US 89 south into Flagstaff. Upon completing Flagstaff, head east on I-40, getting off at Exit 233 and then proceeding six miles south to **Meteor Crater**. This is one of the best preserved meteor impact craters in the world, measuring an awesome 4,100 feet across and almost 600 feet deep. The meteor that created this giant hole in the ground crashed to the earth some 50,000 years ago, but no one realized the crater's origins until about 70 years ago. There is a 3 1/2-mile trail around the crater, but the views are just as good from the platform at the Visitor Center. Smaller examples of meteor rock are on display. Your visit should take under a half-hour. While Meteor Crater is not the greatest attraction on your journey, it is interesting enough to merit a stop. Those who want to see it and still stay with the main itinerary can do so without adding a lot of mileage as it is only about 60 miles round-trip from Flagstaff.

Continue east on I-40 until Exit 311, which brings you to the Petrified Forest National Park, where you can pick up directions for the main route.

FOUR SIDE TRIPS:
To the Grand Canyon's North Rim. One of the biggest mistakes you can make at the South Rim of the Grand Canyon is to skip the North Rim because "it has to be the same." It's not.

The round trip adds about 240 miles of fabulous scenery to the main itinerary and requires two days travel and sightseeing time. It begins along US 89, 23 miles before you get to Page and the Glen Canyon area at the tiny town of Bitter Springs. Branch off of US 89 onto US 89A (or Alternate-89). Your first stop is 14 miles north at **Marble Canyon**. The 616-foot Navajo Bridge crosses the spectacular gorge and there are viewpoints from which you can look into the 800-foot-deep canyon. The colorful pattern of the canyon's walls accounts for its name. East of Marble Canyon, US 89A traverses the equally colorful **Vermillion Cliffs**. Although the colors are most dramatic around sunset (when they can be a fiery red), it is a beautiful sight in any light. The best place to stop for a view is at a roadside pullout 30 miles east of Marble Canyon. From that point it is 11 more miles to the junction of AZ 67 at Jacob Lake, and then 40 more miles south to the North Rim.

The North Rim averages about 1,500 feet higher than the South, so it's considerably cooler. North Rim also refers to the village where the Visitor Center is located, along with food and overnight accommodations at the Grand Canyon Lodge (there is also a motel at Jacob Lake). Make reservations as far in advance as possible since rooms are limited. Visitor facilities are few compared to the South Rim, but that is an advantage as well – you'll feel more as if you are only in the company of nature.

From the Visitor Center there is an easy half-mile round-trip trail to **Bright Angel Point**. This is one of the most remarkable vistas in all of the Grand Canyon as Bright Angel Canyon is joined by two other equally beautiful canyons here. Water can be seen rushing from the cliff walls into the Roaring Spring. Three miles north of the village is where the spectacular **Cape Royal Scenic Drive** begins (leading 20 miles to a dead end). Shortly after beginning the drive there is a short (three-mile) spur leading to Point Imperial – at 8,803 feet, the highest point from which to view the Grand Canyon. The Vermillion Cliffs, distant Navajo Mountain, the Painted Desert, and the Little Colorado River Gorge are all visible from Point Imperial.

Other outstanding places to view the canyon from the Cape Royal Drive are the Vista Encantadora and the Walhala Overlook. At Cape Royal there is another half-mile trail (each way) from the end of the road to the canyon rim. Along the way you'll pass an unusual geologic formation known as the Angel's Window. There are other short and long trails along the rim, but the same rules apply here as on the South Rim for trips that descend into the canyon itself.

Allow a minimum of a half-day to visit the North Rim, including the not insignificant mileage that has to be driven within the Park. After completing your visit just reverse the route back to US 89.

Monument Valley. This side trip covers only about 70 miles and can be done in a half-day or less. From US 160 near the town of Kayenta, take US 163 for 25 miles to **Monument Valley Navajo Tribal Park.** This attraction was described in Chapter 2, as it lies partially in Utah. When you have finished touring Monument Valley, return to the main route just beyond Kayenta.

More of the Sonoran Desert. This is a much longer side trip requiring an additional night to complete, but it's worth the time and effort for anyone who loves the desert. It begins in Tucson, where you should head west on the Tucson-Ajo Highway (AZ 86). In 34 miles you'll reach AZ 386 – turn right and continue for nine miles, climbing through the Quinlan Mountains to the top of 6,875-foot **Kitt Peak,** home of the Kitt Peak National Observatory. Some 20 telescopes are housed in this facility, some of which are so large that you can walk into them. There are both guided and self-guided walking tours of the complex, including a fine Visitor Center with exhibits on all aspects of astronomy and space science. An observation deck located 10 floors above provides outstanding views of the surrounding southern Arizona mountains and desert. It's a lot cooler up here too, which will be a refreshing change from the 100-degree-plus weather you'll probably encounter through most of this side trip. Allow an hour to 90 minutes for your visit to Kitt Peak.

AZ 86 continues through the Sonoran Desert and the Papago Indian Reservation. You'll pass through the town of Why (why it got that name is a mystery), and then take AZ 85 north for 10 miles to the town of Ajo. This is the site of the **Phelps Dodge Mine**, a huge open pit copper mine 1 1/2 miles south of town. The pit is a mile across and 1,000 feet deep. There are several motels in Ajo and it makes the most logical choice of a place to stay along this route.

Head back to Why, staying on AZ 85 for a few miles more until you enter the **Organ Pipe Cactus National Monument**. This is perhaps the best example of a Sonoran Desert environment anywhere in Arizona. Organ Pipe is the name of a particular type of cactus that is similar to the Saguaro, but the branches come from the base of the cactus rather than the vertical shaft. The colorful blossoms of the different cacti are best in March and April (when it's also a lot cooler) but some last through June. The Monument contains a Visitor Center and nature trail where you can get an idea of the various cactus plants that exist within this area. There are also two drives, the 53-mile **Puerto Blanco Scenic Drive** and the 21-mile **Ajo Mountain Drive**. Both are dirt roads and each is a separate one-way loop with no turning back once you begin – so be sure you want to take them before starting. The Ajo Mountain Drive, besides being shorter, provides some nice mountain scenery in addition to the cactus. You can also choose to walk along at least part of the very long Estes Canyon Trail. The Ajo Mountain Drive can be accomplished in about two hours, but the Puerto Blanco takes almost a half-day. Allow about an hour for seeing the sights in the vicinity of the Visitor Center. For those not wishing to stay in Ajo, there is a motel in Lukeville on the Mexican border at the Monument's southern end. It's called the "Gringo Pass Motel"! The route back to Tucson is the exact opposite of the one used to get here. The journey covers about 340 miles, excluding mileage on one or both loops in Organ Pipe Cactus National Monument.

To Arizon's Southeastern Corner. This side trip covers 150 miles round-trip, beginning and rejoining the main itinerary at the town of Benson, just before exiting from I-10 on the way to Tombstone. For this excursion, however, we'll stay on I-10. The first attraction is at Exit 318 in the town of Dragoon.

The **Amerind Foundation Museum** is both a museum and an archeological research center. Over 10,000 years of Indian culture is traced, covering not only the Indians of the American Southwest, but those as far away as the Pacific Northwest and Mexico. Allow a minimum of 45 minutes.

The town of Willcox (Exit 340) contains two brief stops of interest. The **Cochise Visitor Center and Museum** is devoted to the saga of the Apache tribe. The **Rex Allen Arizona Cowboy Museum** tells the life story of local boy Rex Allen who went on to a western film career. You can visit both places in less than an hour. There are a few chain and other motels located in Wilcox adjacent to the Interstate highway.

From the town of Wilcox take AZ 186 for 31 miles to the junction of SR 181 and then follow signs on SR 181 for six miles to the **Chiricahua National Monument**. While this Monument must certainly rank as one of the lesser known and visited of National Park Service areas, its beauty is glorious. The name translates as "Wonderland of Rocks." Maybe that name should be used to let people know just how wonderful a place it is. It is on a mountain that rises to a height of 7,800 feet, towering above the surrounding desert. Giant monolithic rocks, volcanic in origin, have been sculpted by the forces of erosion into fantastic shapes. You can get an idea of that just by reading through a partial list of the names of these formations – the Mushroom, Punch and Judy, the Totem Pole (a remarkable 137-foot-high feature that is only a few feet wide), and the two-million-pound Balanced Rock which rests on a base only four feet thick. Many of the features can be viewed from the six-mile **Bonita Canyon Drive** that rises to a panoramic overlook at 7,000-foot Massai Point. There is also a Visitor Center and you can look in on a pioneer home built in the late 1800s at Faraway Ranch. Short trails include the Rhyolite Canyon Nature Trail (less than a half-mile) and the Massai Point Trail (a half-mile). There are many longer trails that lead to some of the best formations but many of these are difficult. You can at least attempt to do parts of them. Allow a minimum of two hours for your visit to Chiricahua, and significantly more if you are going to be setting out on any of the longer trails.

You won't want to leave, but when you do simply reverse your route back to Benson and continue on with the main itinerary.

A FINAL OPTION: So far we've covered everything but the western third of Arizona. This is a sparsely populated region with fewer attractions. Although there are several places of outstanding natural beauty, it is not so well endowed as the remainder of the state. But there are things worth seeing and it can be covered in a number of ways:

• As a loop from Phoenix, preferably substituting it for another portion of the main itinerary since this would cover a minimum of 400 miles as a round-trip.

• For those driving into Arizona from the west, parts of it can be done on the way into the state, with the remainder seen on the way back. The order doesn't matter.

• You may wish to begin your trip in Phoenix and end it in Las Vegas (a great way to conclude a vacation). If so, the first half of this route will get you part of the way to Las Vegas.

Some of the above options will require you to play around a bit with the map. We'll assume that the trip will begin at Phoenix and return there, but it certainly doesn't have to.

Starting from Phoenix the route is the same as the main itinerary through the Tuzigoot National Monument just south of Oak Creek Canyon. However, at this point continue south on US 89A for about 45 miles to the town of Prescott. The **Granite Dells** are giant boulders of unusual shape that you will find precariously balanced on AZ 89 about four miles north of the town. There are two interesting attractions in town. One is the **Smoki Museum**, with a collection of Indian artifacts. The building is designed to resemble a Pueblo building both on the outside and inside. Allow about a half-hour. The **Sharlot Hall Museum** is a collection of buildings that includes the Governor's Mansion (1864) and a home of the noted Arizona frontiersman John C. Fremont. A number of other structures and exhibits dealing with the history and culture of the area are on the site, which will take about an hour to visit.

From Prescott travel north on AZ 89 (not to be confused with US 89A) until you reach the junction of I-40 at the town of Ash Fork. Take I-40 westbound for 25 miles to Exit 121 and then follow AZ 66. This road more or less parallels the Interstate and was the means of travel through this area before the highway was built. The route is a bit longer but not that much slower and allows you to stop at the **Grand Canyon Caverns**. This is not in any way associated with the National Park. It is a large cave that is entered through the mouth of a fierce looking dinosaur. You then take an elevator down 200 feet where you embark on a 45-minute guided tour. The cave is cool and has lovely formations in a variety of colors.

About 60 miles past the caverns is the town of Kingman. The county seat and largest town in this part of the state, Kingman is the site of the **Mohave Museum of History and Arts**, which documents developments in the Northwestern part of the state. There is also a collection of items that belonged to Kingman-native Andy Devine, and portraits of American presidents and their first ladies. Outdoor mining exhibits complete your visit, which should take between 30 and 45 minutes. As the largest town along I-40, you'll find plenty of places to stay, including Best Westerns, Days Inns, Holiday Inns, TraveLodges and Quality Inns. Restaurants are equally numerous.

When you are ready to leave Kingman a choice has to be made. Those who are using this option as a means to get to or from southern California via I-40, will continue on that route and can take a short detour at Exit 9 to go to Lake Havasu City. Others, heading towards Las Vegas, will get off I-40 at Exit 48 and take US 93 north into Nevada. Finally, those making the complete loop to Phoenix can do either of the above options (or neither), coming back to Kingman and returning to Phoenix by US 93. We'll take a brief look at each of these alternatives.

Lake Havasu City was a sleepy little town on the banks of the Colorado River when the town's founder, Robert McCulloch, got the idea to purchase **London Bridge**. It was transported to Lake Havasu City brick by brick and rebuilt here in 1971. Originally it crossed nothing but sand, but an artificial channel was made so that it now links the town to an island with numerous recreational facilities. An English "town" consisting of attractive shops and restaurants has grown up next to the Bridge, and it makes an interesting way to spend an hour or so. You can walk or drive across the bridge itself, which is really not all that special to look at. (Most tourists confuse it with the architecturally striking Tower Bridge. This one is just a series of graceful arches supporting a flat surface.) Accommodations in Lake Havasu City are plentiful.

US 93 north from Kingman to Vegas traverses about 50 miles of high desert before entering the **Lake Mead National Recreation Area**. Recreational opportunities are abundant here, including taking a 90-minute boat ride on Lake Mead (from the marina on the Nevada side of the border). The border between Arizona and Nevada runs through the middle of the magnificent **Hoover Dam**, built in the classic style that people visualize when they think of dams. The 726-foot-high structure was completed in 1936. From the top there are beautiful views of the gorge of the Colorado River on the south side, and of the brilliant blue Lake Mead to the north, surrounded by red colored cliffs. Elevators carry visitors down to the bottom where 40-minute guided tours of the power house are given. Expect long lines unless you get there early in the day. The scenery on the way to the dam is some of the best on this entire route as you pass through mountains of varying colors, with the road dropping from the high plateau to the top of the dam. The scenery is even better on the Nevada side of the border, as the changes in elevation of the road are greater and the turns more dramatic. From there it is under an hour into Las Vegas.

And now for those coming back to Phoenix from Kingman. About 20 miles east of Kingman, take Exit 71 off I-40 onto US 93 southbound. It's about 160 miles from this point to Phoenix, and virtually the entire distance is through desert. US 93 is known as the Joshua Tree Parkway, because it goes through areas that contain this unique specimen. They're concentrated in a 20-mile or so stretch of US 93 falling between the junctions of AZ 97 and AZ 71. You can pull off the road in a number of places to read the informational displays about the trees. Before you reach this area be sure to take a quick look at the town of Nothing – and that's exactly what you'll see. (We apologize to the residents – or maybe it should be resident, but we just couldn't help ourselves.)

One last stop can be made before you reach the final home stretch into Phoenix. This is in the town of Wickenburg where the **Desert Caballeros Western Museum** will introduce you to the town's history through attractive dioramas and a recreated street scene, among other exhibits. Allow about 45 minutes.

Itinerary Outlines, Trip Combinations

One purpose of this section is to summarize at a glance the places visited in each of the three suggested state routes, as well as to graphically depict the alternative routings and side trips. Some will find it easier, after having read the preceding chapters, to get a quick picture of the possibilities by making note of their destination choices from these lists. Use these lists along with the state maps in each chapter, or better still, with a detailed road map. The main itinerary runs down the center of each chart, with alternative routes and side trips indicated to the left or right of the primary route. Finally, beneath each chart are suggestions for points where multi-state combinations are best linked together and the mileage you'll have to drive to complete those links.

COLORADO

Alternative Routes	Main Itinerary Outline	Loops & Other Side Trips	
	Denver	(A)	(B)
	Boulder	Loveland	Idaho Springs
	Estes Park	Ft. Collins	Central City
	Rocky Mountain Natl Park	Greeley	
Steamboat Springs	Granby		
Craig	Georgetown		
Rifle	Vail		
	Leadville		
	Aspen		
	Glenwood Springs		
	Grand Junction	Grand Mesa/Lands End	
	Colorado Natl Monument		
	Montrose		
Curecanti	Black Canyon of Gunnison		
Gunnison	Ouray/Million Dollar Hwy		
	Durango		
	Mesa Verde Natl Park		
	Durango	Alamosa	
	Salida	Great Sand Dunes (Antonito)	
	Canon City		
	Colorado Springs	Florrisant Fossil Beds	
	Denver	Cripple Creek	

Combining Colorado with other State Itineraries:
(1) From the western end of the Colorado National Monument, take I-70 west across into Utah, Exit #212 at the town of Cisco. This joins with the main Utah itinerary, beginning with the scenic drive on UT 128. The distance between the two itineraries is 41 miles.

(2) From Mesa Verde National Park, proceed 10 miles west to Cortez. From there you may:

(a) Take US 160 (west) past Four Corners Monument to eight miles east of Kayenta, Arizona, a distance of 109 miles. This links with the main Arizona itinerary on the way to Canyon de Chelly National Monument. Or...

(b) Continue as above, 10 miles past Kayenta and do the Monument Valley side trip, where you can also link with the primary Utah route.

UTAH

Alternative Routes	Main Itinerary Outline	Loops & Other Side Trips	
Heber City	Salt Lake City	(A)	(B)
Vernal	Helper/Spring Canyon	Alta/Brighton	Brigham City
Dinosaur Natl Mon	Price	Golden Spike	Park City
Flaming Gorge	Green River/Gray Canyon	NHS	Ogden
Natl Rec Area	Utah 128		
Duchesne	Moab		(C)
	Arches/Canyonlands	La Sal Mtn	Great Salt
	Blanding		Lake & Desert
	Monument Valley		Bonneville
	Natural Bridges Natl Mon		Flats
	Capitol Reef Natl Park		
	Boulder-Escalante		
	Bryce Canyon Natl Park	Kanab	
	Zion National Park	(Page/Glen Canyon)	
	St. George	(Grand Canyon-	
	Cedar City/Cedar Breaks	North Rim)	
	Fillmore		
	Provo		
	Alpine Scenic Loop		
	Salt Lake City		

Combining Utah with other State Itineraries:
(1) From I-70's Exit #202 (Cisco), continue for 41 miles on I-70 eastbound to the Colorado National Monument Exit (the reverse of Colorado Link (1).

(2) From Monument Valley, take US 163 south for 24 miles (just past Kayenta) to the junction of US 160, where it links with the main Arizona itinerary, again heading to Canyon de Chelly. You

also have the opportunity to stay on US 160 all the way into Cortez, Colorado to link with that trip at Mesa Verde National Park.

(3) From Kanab, head south on US 89 for 74 miles to the town of Page and pick up the Arizona itinerary with Glen Canyon National Recreation Area; or take US 89A south from Kanab for 37 miles to Jacob Lake, where you'll join the Grand Canyon North Rim side trip. (This can also be reached via UT 59 and AZ 389 and then US 89A from the town of Hurricane, located 10 miles east of St. George. The total distance coming from this point is 82 miles.)

ARIZONA

Alternative Routes	Main Itinerary Outline	Loops & Other Side Trips
	Phoenix	Prescott
	Mesa/Tempe/Scottsdale	Grand Canyon Caverns
	Sedona/Oak Creek Canyon	Kingman – Lake Havasu or
Meteor Crater/		Lake Mead/Las Vegas
Winslow	Flagstaff	
	Wupatki/Walnut Canyon Loop	
	Grand Canyon (South)	
	Cameron	Grand Canyon-North Rim
	Page	
	Kayenta	Monument Valley
	Glen Canyon Natl Rec Area	
	Canyon de Chelly Natl Mn	
	Petrified Forest Natl Park	
The Apache Trail	Globe	
	Tucson	Kitt Peak
	Saguaro Natl Monument	Dragoon	Sonoran Desert
	Tombstone	Wilcox	Organ Pipe
	Sierra Vista	Chiricahua	Cactus Natl Mn
	Nogales	Natl Mn	
	Tumacacori NHS/Tubac Presidio	
	Tucson	
	Phoenix	

Combining Arizona with other State Itineraries:

Rather than repeating the information contained under Colorado and Utah, the easiest way to look at the links available from Arizona is to reverse Colorado Link (2) or Utah Links (2) and (3).

Addendum 2

Quick Reference Attraction Index

This listing will refer you to the pages where each attraction is described. In addition, it provides information on its hours of operation and admission fees. The list is in alphabetical order, by state. The last column indicates where a description can be found.

HOURS: The hours listed are for the summer months, generally June through September. If traveling at other times of the year it is a good idea to check on the possibility of reduced hours. When no times are given, the attraction is open all the time, or at least during daylight hours. Visitor Centers in National and State Parks are usually open from 8:00 or 9:00 a.m. until at least 5:00 p.m., although the parks themselves do not close or have much longer hours.

PRICES: The number indicates the full adult admission price, rounded to the next highest dollar, based on prices at time of publication. Thus, these figures are for reference purposes only. Discounts for children or senior citizens are usually available. National and state parks generally do not have a per person admission price; rather, there is a fee for each car entering. The fee is waived in the National Parks for persons who present a Golden Eagle or Golden Age Passport. This type of fee area is indicated by a dollar sign ($) in the listing. The letter "D" indicates donations in lieu of fixed admission prices.

COLORADO

Attraction, Hours	$ Cost	Book Page
Alamosa National Wildlife Refuge	Free	43
American Numismatic Museum, Mon-Fri 8:30-4; Sat 9-4	1	32
Anheuser-Busch Brewery, daily 9:30-5	Free	38
Argo Gold Mill, daily 10-7	10	39
Astor House Hotel, Tues-Sat 10-4	1	13
Bachelor-Syracuse Mine, daily 9-5	8	26
Bar-D Chuckwagon, evenings	$	27
Betty Ford Alpine Garden	Free	21
Black Canyon of the Gunnison	$	25

Attraction, Hours	$ Cost	Book Page
Box Canyon, daily 8-8	2	26
Broadmoor, The	Free	32
Brown Palace Hotel	Free	12
Buckskin Joe, daily 8-dusk	2	30
Buffalo Bill Memorial Museum, daily 9-5	2	14
Buffalo Bill Wax Museum, daily 9-9	4	34
Byers-Evans House, Wed-Mon 11-3	3	11
Cave of the Winds, daily 9-8	3	34
Cheesman Park	Free	12
Cheyenne Mountain Zoo, daily 9-6	6	33
Chimney Rock	Free	29
City Park	Free	12
Civic Center	Free	9
Classic Victorian Melodrama, Tue-Sat at noon & 7; Sun noon & 4	10	42
Colorado 103 (State Highway)	Free	39
Colorado History Museum, Mon-Sat 10-4:30; Sun 12-4:30	3	11
Colorado National Monument	$	24
Colorado Railroad Museum, daily 9-5	3	14
Colorado School of Mines Museum, Mon-Sat 9-4	Free	39
Colorado Ski Museum/Hall of Fame, Tue-Sun 10-5	1	21
Coors Brewery, Mon-Sat 10-4	Free	13
Cripple Creek & Victor Narrow Gauge Railway, daily 9:30-5:30	6	41
Cripple Creek Museum, daily 9:30-5	2	41
Cumbres & Toltec Scenic Railroad, daily at 10	46	46
Curecanti National Recreation Area, Boat rides daily at 10 &12:30	$	44
Denver Art Museum, Tue-Sat 10-5	3	9
Denver Botanic Gardens, daily 9-4:45	4	13
Denver Museum of Natural History, daily 9-5	4	12
Denver Zoo, daily 10-6	4	12
Diamond Circle Melodrama, Mon-Sat at 8pm	10	27
Durango & Silverton Narrow Gauge Railroad, daily at 8:30 & 9:30am	38	27
Earth Runs Silver, The, daily 10-5	4	21
Edgar Mine, Tue-Sat 8:30-4	4	39
Elitch Gardens, daily 10am-11pm	8+	13
El Pomar Carriage House Museum, Tue-Sun 10-noon, 1-5	Free	32
Estes Park Area Historical Museum, Mon-Sat 10-5; Sun 1-5	1	17
Fish Creek Falls	Free	43
Flagstaff Scenic Highway (Boulder)	Free	16
Florissant Fossil Beds, daily 8-7	$	41
Fort Collins Museum, Tue-Sat 10-5; Sun 12-5	Free	38
Fort Uncompahgre, Wed-Sun 10-5	2	25
Fort Vasquez, Mon-Sat 10-5; Sun 1-5	Free	39
Garden of the Gods	D	35
Georgetown Loop Historic Mining Area Train, daily 9:20-4	11	20
Grand Mesa/Lands End	Free	44
Grant-Humphreys Mansion, Tue-Fri 10-2	2	11
Great Sand Dunes National Monument	$	46
Hall of Presidents Wax Museum, daily 9-9	4	35

Attraction, Hours	$ Cost	Book Page
Hamill House, daily 10-5	3	20
Hanging Lake	Free	23
Healy House, daily 10-4:30	3	21
Heritage Museum (Leadville), daily 10-6	3	21
Historic Centennial Village, Tue-Sat 10-5; Sun 1-5	3	38
Hotel de Paris, daily 9-5	3	20
Independence Ghost Town	Free	23
Leadville, Colorado & Southern Railroad Co., daily 9:30 and 2	17	22
Lime Creek Canyon	Free	27
Lookout Mountain Park	Free	14
Loveland Museum, Tue-Fri 10-5; Sat 10-4; Sun 12-4	1	38
MacGregor Ranch & Museum, Tue-Sat 11-5	D	17
Manitou Cliff Dwellings Museum, daily 9-7	4	34
Maroon Bells, buses leave daily 9-4:30	4	23
Mesa Verde National Park	$	28
Michael Ricker Museum & Gallery, daily 9-9	Free	17
Million Dollar Highway	Free	26
Mollie Kathleen Gold Mine, daily 9-5	7	42
Molly Brown House, Mon-Sat 10-4; Sun 12-4	3	11
Mother Cabrini Shrine	Free	14
Mt. Shavano State Fish Hatchery, daily 8-4	D	30
National Center for Atmospheric Rsrch, Mon-Fri 8-5; Sat & Sun 9-3	Free	16
National Mining Hall of Fame & Museum, daily 9-5	3	22
North Cheyenne Canyon/High Drive	Free	33
Northwest Colorado, Museum of (Craig), Mon-Sat 10-4	D	43
Opera House (Central City), daily 11:30-4	3	40
Pearce-McAllister Cottage, Tue-Sat 10-4; Sun 1-4	3	11
Peterson Air & Space Museum, Tue-Fri 8:30-4:30; Sat 9:30-4:30	Free	31
Pikes Peak Cog Railway, daily 8-5:20	21	35
Pro Rodeo Hall of Fame, daily 9-5	5	36
Red Rocks Park	Free	13
events	$	
Rio Grande County Museum, Mon-Sat 10-5	1	30
Rocky Mountain National Park	$	18
Royal Gorge Bridge	9	30
St. Mary's Glacier	Free	40
Santa's Workshop-North Pole, daily 9:30-6	8	41
Seven Falls, daily 8am-11pm	7	33
Shrine of the Sun, daily 9-5	$	33
Skyline Drive	Free	31
State Capitol, Mon-Fri 9-2:30	Free	11
Steamboat Springs Ski Area & Gondola, daily 9-4	10	42
Strater Hotel	Free	27
Tabor House, daily 9-5	2	22
Tabor Opera House, Sun-Fri 9-5:30	3	22
Taylor Reservoir	Free	44
Teller House, daily 8am-2am	3	40
Trinity United Methodist Church, Mon-Fri 8-5	Free	11
United States Air Force Academy, Visitor Center daily 9-6	Free	36
United States Mint, Mon-Fri 8-3 (Wed 9-3)	Free	9
United States Olympic Complex, Mon-Sat 9-5; Sun 10-4	Free	32

Attraction, Hours	$ Cost	Book Page
Hansen Planetarium, Mon-Thu 9-3; Fri & Sat 9am-Midnight; Sun 1-4	6	53
Heber Valley Historic Railroad, daily 10 & 2:30	16	80
Hill Aerospace Museum, Tue-Fri 9-3; Sat & Sun 9-5:30	D	78
Hole in the Rock, daily 9-6	2	59
Hotel Utah, Mon-Fri 8-4:30	Free	52
Inspiration Point	Free	86
Jacob Hamlin House, daily 8:30-8	Free	70
John Wesley Powell Museum of River History, daily 8-8	D	57
Kodachrome Basin State Park	$	66
Kolob Canyon (section of Zion National Park)	$	71
Lagoon Amusement Park, daily 11-11	17	78
La Sal Mountains Loop Road	Free	83
Liberty Park	Free	55
McCurdy Doll Museum, Tue-Sat 12-6	2	73
Monument Valley Navajo Tribal Park, daily 8-6	1	63
Moqui Cave, Mon-Sat 8:30-7	3	85
Natural Bridges National Monument	$	64
Needles Overlook (Canyonlands National Park)	Free	84
Newspaper Rock State Historic Monument	Free	84
Park City	Free	77
Park City Museum, Mon-Sat 10-7; Sun 12-6	Free	77
Pioneer Museum (Vernal), Mon-Sat 12-7	Free	81
Pioneer Trail State Park, daily 8-8	$	53
Price Municipal Building, Mon-Fri 8-5	Free	56
Price Prehistoric Museum, Mon-Sat 10-6; Sun 12-5	D	56
Provo Temple	Free	73
Rainbow Bridge Natl Monument, see Arizona		
Red Canyon	Free	82
Red Fleet State Park	$	82
St. George Tabernacle, daily 11-5	Free	70
St. George Temple, daily 8am-10pm	Free	70
Salt Lake Arts Center, Mon-Sat 10-5; Sun 1-5	D	54
Salt Lake City-Council Hall, Mon-Fri 8-5	Free	49
Salt Palace, events	$	54
San Rafael Swell	Free	57
Saratoga Resort, daily 11-8	7+	73
Snow Canyon State Park	$	71
Spring Canyon	Free	56
State Capitol, Mon-Fri 8-4:30	Free	49
Symphony Hall, events	$	54
Temple Square (Ogden)	Free	78
Temple Square (Salt Lake City)	Free	51
Territorial State House State Park, daily 9-6	1	73
Timpanogos Cave National Monument, daily 7-5	5	75
Trolley Square	N/A	54
Union Station Museums, Mon-Sat 10-6; Sun 1-5	2	78
University of Utah, Museum hours vary	Free	53
Utah 128 (State Highway)	Free	58
Utah Field House of Natural History, daily 8-7	1	81
Utah Fine Arts Museum, Mon-Fri 10-5; Sat & Sun 2-5	Free	53
Utah Lake State Park	$	74
Utah Shakespearean Festival, Greenshow	Free	71
Stage Events	$	

Attraction, Hours	$ Cost	Book Page
Heard Museum, Mon-Sat 10-5; Sun 12-5	5	93
Heritage Square	Free	92
Historama, daily 9-4	2	114
Hoover Dam, daily 8-6:45	1	127
Horse, Museum of the, daily 9-5	3	116
Hubbell Trading Post, daily 8-6	Free	106
International Wildlife Museum, daily 9-5:30	5	111
John C. Fremont House, Wed-Sat 10-4	Free	110
John Wesley Powell Museum, Mon-Sat 8-6; Sun 10-6	Free	105
Kitt Peak National Observatory, daily 9-3:45	Free	122
Lake Mead National Recreation Area	Free	127
Boat rides 5 times daily	12+	
Little Colorado River Gorge	Free	103
London Bridge	Free	126
Marble Canyon/Navajo Bridge	Free	121
Mesa Southwest Museum, Tue-Sat 10-5; Sun 1-5	4	96
Meteor Crater, daily 6-6	6	120
Mile High Ramsey Canyon Preserve	Free	115
Mission San Xavier del Bac, daily 8-6	D	117
Mohave Museum of History & Arts		
Mon-Fri 10-5; Sat & Sun 1-5	1	126
Montezuma Castle National Monument, daily 8-7	1	98
Monument Valley, see Utah listing		
Mystery Castle, Tue-Sun 11-5	3	93
Navajo National Monument	Free	105
Northern Arizona, Museum of, daily 9-5	4	100
Oak Creek Canyon	Free	99
O.K. Corral, daily 8:30-5	2	114
Old Tucson Studios, daily 9-9	11	111
Organ Pipe Cactus National Monument	$	123
Painted Desert Vista	Free	101
Petrified Forest National Park	$	107
Phelps Dodge Copper Mine	Free	123
Phoenix Art Museum, Tue-Sat 10-5 (Wed to 9pm)	4	93
Sun 12-5		
Phoenix Zoo, daily 7-4	6	94
Pima Air & Space Museum, daily 9-5	5	112
Pueblo Grande Museum, Mon-Sat 9-4:45; Sun 1-4:45	1	94
Rainbow Bridge National Monument	N/A	86
(included in boat ride)		
Rawhide, Mon-Fri 5pm-10pm; Sat & Sun		
11am-10pm, rides	2	97
Riordan State Historic Park, daily 9-5	3	100
Rose Tree Inn Museum, daily 8-5	2	115
Rosson House, Wed-Sat 10-3:30; Sun 12-4	3	92
Sabino Canyon	Free	112
Saguaro Natl Monument, East Unit	$	111
West Unit	$	
Salt River Canyon	Free	108
Scottsdale Civic Center & Mall	Free	96
Sentinel Peak Park	Free	110
Sharlot Hall Museum, Tue-Sat 10-5; Sun 1-5	D	125
Silver Nugget Museum, The, daily 9-5	2	115
Smoki Museum, Mon, Tue, Th-Sat 10-5; Sun 1-5	D	125
Snow Bowl, daily 10-5	8	100

Addendum 3

For Further Information

General State & City Information

COLORADO
Colorado Tourism Board
PO Box 38700
Denver CO 80238
(800) 433-2656

Denver Convention & Visitors Bureau
225 W. Colfax Avenue
Denver CO 80202
(800) 265-6723

Colorado Springs Visitor Bureau
104 S. Cascade
Colorado Springs CO 80903
(719) 635-7506

UTAH
Utah Travel Council
Council Hall/Capitol Hill
Salt Lake City UT 84114
(801) 538-1030

Salt Lake City Convention & Visitors Bureau
180 S. West Temple Street
Salt Lake City UT 84101
(801) 521-2868

ARIZONA
Arizona Office of Tourism
1100 W. Washington Street
Phoenix AZ 85007
(602) 542-8687

Phoenix & Valley of the Sun Convention & Visitors Bureau
122 N. 2nd Street
Phoenix AZ 85004
(602) 254-6400

Metropolitan Tucson Convention & Visitors Bureau
130 S. Scott Avenue
Tucson AZ 85701
(602) 624-1817

National Park Service Facilities

Address all written inquiries to the SUPERINTENDENT of the
particular facility at the addresses below.

COLORADO
Black Canyon of the Gunnison National Monument
2233 East Main
Montrose CO 81402
(303) 249-7036

Colorado National Monument
Fruita CO 81521
(303) 858-3617

Curecanti National Recreation Area
102 Elk Creek
Gunnison CO 81230
(303) 641-2337

Florissant Fossil Beds National Monument
PO Box 185
Florissant CO 80816
(303) 748-3253

Mesa Verde National Park
Mesa Verde National Park CO 81330
(303) 529-4465

Rocky Mountain National Park
Estes Park CO 80517
(303) 586-2371

UTAH
Arches National Park
PO Box 907
Moab UT 84532
(801) 259-8161

Bryce Canyon National Park
Bryce Canyon UT 84717
(801) 834-5322

Canyonlands National Park
125 W. 200 South
Moab UT 84532
(801) 259-7164

Capitol Reef National Park
Torrey UT84795
(801) 425-3791

Cedar Breaks National Monument
PO Box 749
Cedar City UT 84720
(801) 586-9451

Golden Spike National Historic Site
PO Box W
Brigham City UT 84302
(801) 471-2209

Rainbow Bridge National Monument
See Glen Canyon NRA, Arizona for details

Timpanogos Cave National Monument
Rural Route 3, Box 200
American Fork UT 84003
(801) 756-5238

ARIZONA
Canyon de Chelly National Monument
PO Box 588
Chinle AZ 86503
(602) 674-5436

Casa Grande Ruins National Monument
1100 Ruins Drive
Coolidge AZ 85228
(602) 723-3172

Chiracahua National Monument
Dos Cabezas Drive
PO Box 6500
Willcox AZ 85643
(602) 824-3560

Glen Canyon National Recreation Area
PO Box 1507
Page AZ 86040
(602) 645-8200
For boat tours, call: (800) 528-6154

Grand Canyon National Park
PO Box 129
Grand Canyon AZ 86023
(602) 638-7888

Hubbell Trading Post National Historic Site
PO Box 150
Ganado AZ 86505
(602) 755-3475

Lake Mead National Recreation Area
601 Nevada Highway
Boulder City NV 89005
(702) 293-8907
For boat tours, call: (702) 293-6180

Montezuma Castle National Monument
PO Box 219
Camp Verde AZ 86322
(602) 567-3322

Navajo National Monument
HC 71 Box 3
Tonalea AZ 86044
(602) 672-2366

Organ Pipe Cactus National Monument
Route 1, Box 100
Ajo AZ 85321
(602) 387-6849

Petrified Forest National Park
PO Box 2217
Petrified Forest National Park AZ 86028
(602) 524-6228

Saguaro National Monument
3693 S. Old Spanish Trail
Tucson AZ 85230
(602) 296-8576

Sunset Crater National Monument
Route 3, Box 149
Flagstaff AZ 86004
(602) 527-7042

Tumacacori National Historic Park
PO Box 67
Tumacacori AZ 85640
(602) 398-2341

Tuzigoot National Monument
PO Box 68
Clarkdale AZ 86324
(602) 634-5564

Walnut Crater National Monument
Walnut Crater Road
Flagstaff AZ 86004
(602) 526-3367

Wupatki National Monument
2717 N. Steves Blvd., Suite 3
Flagstaff AZ 86001
(602) 527-7134

Lodging

Within National Parks

Mesa Verde National Park
ARA Mesa Verde
PO Box 277
Mancos CO 81328
(303) 529-4421

Bryce Canyon, Zion and
North Rim of Grand Canyon
TW Recreational Services Inc.
PO Box 400
Cedar City UT 84720
(801) 586-7686

Grand Canyon (South Rim)
The Grand Canyon National Park Lodges
c/o Fred Harvey Company
PO Box 699
Grand Canyon AZ 86023
(602) 638-2401

Glen Canyon National Recreation Area
ARA Leisure Services
Lake Powell Resorts & Marinas
2916 N. 35th Ave., Suite 8
Phoenix AZ 85017
(800) 528-6154

Major Hotel Chains
Toll-Free Reservation & Information numbers:

Best Western International	(800) 528-1234
Choice Hotels:	
Clarion Hotels	(800) 221-2222
Comfort Inn	(800) 221-2222
EconoLodge	(800) 424-4777
Friendship Inns	(800) 424-4777
Quality Inns	(800) 221-2222
Rodeway Inns	(800) 424-4777
Days Inn	(800) 325-2525
Hilton Hotels	(800) 445-8667

Holiday Inns	(800) 465-4329
Howard Johnson Motor Lodges/ HoJo Inns	(800) 446-4656
La Quinta Motor Inns	(800) 531-5900
Marriott Hotels	(800) 228-9290
Ramada Inns	(800) 228-2828
Red Lion/Thunderbird Motor Inns	(800) 547-8010
Sheraton Hotels	(800) 325-3535
Super 8 Motels	(800) 843-1991
Travelodge	(800) 255-3050

Locations of Major Chains in the Region
indicates more than one

BEST WESTERN
(Colorado)
Alamosa, Basalt (Aspen), Boulder*, Canon City, Colorado Springs, Cortez*, Craig, Cripple Creek, Delta, Denver*, Dillon, Durango*, Eagle, Estes Park*, Fort Collins, Frisco, Glenwood Springs*, Grand Junction*, Greeley, Gunnison, Loveland, Monte Vista, Montrose, Ouray, Pagosa Springs, Salida, Steamboat Springs, Vail, Wheat Ridge (Denver)

(Utah)
Beaver*, Blanding, Bryce Canyon (Ruby's Inn), Cedar City*, Fillmore, Green River, Hurricane, Kanab, Logan*, Moab*, Monticello, Mt. Carmel Jct., Nephi, Ogden*, Panguitch, Park City, Parowan, Provo*, Roosevelt, St. George*, Salt Lake City*, Springdale, Torrey, Vernal, Wendover

(Arizona)
Benson, Camp Verde, Casa Grande, Chambers, Cottonwood, Flagstaff*, Glendale (Phoenix), Goodyear (Phoenix), Grand Canyon (South Rim), Holbrook*, Kingman*, Lake Havasu City, Mesa*, Miami (Globe), Nogales, Page*, Phoenix*, Pine Top, Prescott, Scottsdale*, Sedona, Show Low, Snowflake, Sun City (Phoenix), Tombstone, Tucson*, Wickenburg, Willcox, Winslow*

CHOICE
Clarion Hotels
(Colorado)
Boulder, Englewood (Denver) CO

(Utah)
Salt Lake City

(Arizona)
Prescott

Comfort/Sleep Inns
(Colorado)
Avon, Colorado Springs, Cortez, Denver*, Durango, Lakewood (Denver), Estes Park, Fort Collins, Monte Vista

(Utah)
Beaver, Blanding, Cedar Cotu, Logan, Moab, Price, Provo, Salt Lake City*,
Sandy, St. George*, South Jordan

(Arizona)
Flagstaff, Holbrook, Phoenix*, Prescott, Tempe, Tucson, Willcox, Williams

ECONO LODGE
(Colorado)
Colorado Springs, Denver*, Durango, Fort Collins

(Utah)
Cedar City, Green River, Salt Lake City, Vernal

(Arizona)
Flagstaff*, Holbrook, Page, Phoenix, Pine Top, Tempe, Williams, Winslow

FRIENDSHIP INNS
(Colorado)
Grand Jct., Gunnison, Salida

QUALITY INNS/SUITES
(Colorado)
Colorado Springs, Denver

(Utah)
Beaver, Cedar City, Richfield, Salt Lake City*

(Arizona)
Cottonwood, Flagstaff*, Grand Canyon (Tusayan), Green Valley, Kingman, Mesa,
Phoenix*, Sedona, Tempe, Williams

RODEWAY INNS
(Colorado)
Colorado Springs, Lakewood (Denver)

(Arizona)
Flagstaff*, Kingman, Mesa, Phoenix*, Scottsdale, Tempe, Tucson*, Williams

DAYS INN
(Colorado)
Alamosa, Boulder, Canon City, Carbondale, Colorado Springs, Cortez, Denver*,
Dillon, Durango, Fort Collins, Golden (Denver), Gunnison, Montrose, Salida

(Utah)
Cedar City, Logan, Moab, Monticello, Price, Provo, Salt Lake City, St. George*,
Vernal

(Arizona)
Ash Fork, Flagstaff*, Holbrook, Kingman*, Lake Havasu City, Mesa, Phoenix*, Prescott, Scottsdale, Show Low, Tempe, Tucson, Williams, Winslow

HILTON
(Colorado)
Breckenridge, Colorado Springs, Denver (Englewood), Grand Junction

(Utah)
St. George, Salt Lake City*

(Arizona)
Mesa, Phoenix*, Scottsdale, Tucson

HOLIDAY INN
(Colorado)
Alamosa, Aurora (Denver), Boulder, Colorado Springs*, Cortez, Craig, Cripple Creek, Denver*, Durango, Estes Park, Fort Collins*, Frisco, Glenwood Springs, Golden (Denver), Grand Junction, Greeley, Lakewood (Denver), Steamboat Springs, Vail

(Utah)
Cedar City, Ogden, Provo, Salt Lake City*, St. George

(Arizona)
Casa Grande, Chinle, Flagstaff*, Holbrook, Kayenta, Kingman, Lake Havasu City, Mesa, Page, Phoenix*, Scottsdale*, Tempe, Tucson*, Williams

HOWARD JOHNSON
(Colorado)
Colorado Springs, Denver*, Grand Junction, Silverthorne

(Utah)
Brigham City, Salina, Salt Lake City

(Arizona)
Flagstaff*, Lake Havasu City, Phoenix, Scottsdale*, Tempe, Tucson*, Williams

MARRIOTT
Marriott Hotels
(Colorado)
Colorado Springs, Denver*, Golden (Denver), Fort Collins

(Utah)
Salt Lake City

(Arizona)
Scottsdale*

Residence Inns
(Colorado)
Boulder, Colorado Springs, Denver*

(Utah)
Salt Lake City*

(Arizona)
Flagstaff, Phoenix, Scottsdale, Tempe, Tucson

Courtyard By Marriott
(Colorado)
Boulder, Denver*

(Arizona)
Mesa, Phoenix*, Scottsdale, Tucson

Fairfield Inns
(Colorado)
Denver

(Utah)
Provo

(Arizona)
Flagstaff, Phoenix*, Scottsdale

RAMADA INN
(Colorado)
Colorado Springs*, Cortez, Denver*, Fort Collins, Glenwood Springs, Grand Junction, Gunnison, Lakewood (Denver), Westminster (Denver)

(Utah)
Moab, Salt Lake City, St. George

(Arizona)
Holbrook, Phoenix*, Scottsdale, Sierra Vista, Tempe, Tucson*, Williams

SHERATON
(Colorado)
Denver*, Lakewood (Denver), Steamboat Springs, Thornton (Denver)

(Arizona)
Chandler (Phoenix), Mesa, Phoenix, Prescott, Tempe, Tucson

SUPER 8
(Colorado)
Boulder, Brighton (Denver), Canon City, Castle Rock, Colorado Springs*, Cortez, Craig, Denver*, Dillon, Durango, Fort Collins, Grand Junction, Gunnison, Longmont*, Loveland, Montrose, Pagosa Springs, Parachute, Salida, Steamboat Springs

(Utah)
Cedar City, Green River, Logan, Moab, Nephi, Ogden, Park City, Provo, St. George, Salt Lake City

(Arizona)
Camp Verde, Chandler (Phoenix), Eloy, Flagstaff, Goodyear (Phoenix), Holbrook, Kingman, Lake Havasu City, Mesa, Nogales, Page, Phoenix*, Prescott, Scottsdale, Sedona, Sierra Vista, Tempe, Tucson, Williams, Winslow

Major National Car Rental Companies

Alamo	(800) 327-9633	Enterprise	(800) 325-8007
Avis	(800) 321-1212	Hertz	(800) 654-3131
Budget	(800) 527-0700	National	(800) 227-7368
Dollar	(800) 421-6868	Thrifty	(800) 367-2277

Additional Reading

Other travel guides from Hunter Publishing

ADVENTURE GUIDE TO THE HIGH SOUTHWEST
Steve Cohen
A guide to hiking, mountaineering, trail riding, cycling, camping, river running, ski touring, wilderness trips, and the area's natural attractions for the outdoor-minded. Includes all practical details on transportation, services, where to eat, where to stay. Focusses on the Four Corners of NW New Mexico, SW Colorado, Southern Utah, Northern Arizona, the Navajo Nation and Hopiland. Maps. *380-page paperback/$14.95/1-55650-633-3*

WHERE TO STAY IN THE AMERICAN SOUTHWEST
Phil Philcox
A definitive guide, this describes virtually every hotel, motel, and B&B in the region, with at least 5,000 places to bed down for the night covered. From a Motel 6 on the highway to a historic house with three rooms for guests and complimentary breakfast to all the giant downtown hotels, more places by far are detailed here than in any other guide to the area. Includes Texas, Oklahoma, New Mexico, Colorado, Arizona, Nevada, Utah. Maps. *500-page paperback/$13.95/1-55650652-X*

CANADIAN ROCKIES ACCESS GUIDE
John Dodd & Gail Helgason
The ultimate adventure, from Banff to Lake Louise to Jasper National Park. Walking, hiking, canoeing routes, cycling suggestions. Maps, photos. *360-page paperback/$15.95/0-919433-92-8*

THE GREAT AMERICAN WILDERNESS
Larry H. Ludmer
The most scenic parks, from Acadia to Yosemite, and how to see them. Access routes, where to stay and eat, the most beautiful spots, what to see if time is short, plus what you can safely skip. Includes maps of each park and detailed itineraries for driving. *300-page paperback/$11.95/1-55650-567-1*

ADVENTURE GUIDE TO BAJA CALIFORNIA 2nd Ed.
Wilbur H. Morrison
Thorough update of this highly successful guide to touring Baja, from Tijuana and Mexicali in the north to Cabo San Lucas at the

southern tip. The best driving routes, fascinating history, hotels, restaurants, all practical details. Maps. *320-page paperback/$13.95/1-55650-590-6*

ADVENTURE GUIDE TO THE EVERGLADES & FLORIDA KEYS
Joyce & Jon Huber
Fishing, hiking, diving, relaxing in south Florida. Everything to see and do, from the wilderness canoe trails of the Everglades to the bizarre sights of Key West. Maps & color photos. *224-page paperback/$14.95/1-55650-494-2*

ADVENTURE GUIDE TO THE ALASKA HIGHWAY
Ed & Lynn Readicker-Henderson
Everything you need to know about driving the highway, plus all worthwhile sidetrips from and approaches to the route, including the Alaska Marine Highway, Klondike Highway, Top-of-the-World Highway. Maps & color photos. *288-page paperback/$15.95/1-55650-457-8*

CRUISING ALASKA: A TRAVELLER'S GUIDE TO CRUISING ALASKAN WATERS AND EXPLORING THE INTERIOR
Larry H. Ludmer
Filled with concise profiles of all the ships that cruise Alaskan waters, with stateroom size, the latest prices and amenities, this book also describes each port of call, providing maps, information sources, restaurants, local festivities, and entertainment. The guide then takes a step further, with excursions to Denali and other National Parks. *256-page paperback/$14.95/1-55650-650-3*

ADVENTURE GUIDE TO COSTA RICA 2nd Ed.
Harry S. Pariser
The biggest, most detailed guide on the market. "This is the one to take with you on your next trip. May be the best-balanced, most comprehensive of the entire bunch. Excellent sections on the national parks, flora and fauna, and history. " *Great Expeditions.* "This extensive, up-to-date guide is a welcome sight. Accommodations and restaurants span the scale from luxury to low budget, while the respectful, ecologically aware perspective contributes a progressive view of the mountains, lowlands, rain forests, and beaches." *American Library Association Booklist. Maps & color photos. 360-page paperback/$15.95/1-55650-598-1*